KU-764-352

Crossway Bible Guide

Series Editors: Ian Coffey (NT), Stephen Gaukroger (OT)
New Testament Editor: Stephen Motyer

Also in this series

Exodus: Stephen Dray

Acts: Crossway Bible Guide

Free to Live

Stephen Gaukroger

Crossway Books
Nottingham

Copyright © 1993 by Stephen Gaukroger

First edition 1993

All rights reserved.
No part of this publication may be reproduced or transmitted in
any form or by any means, electronic, or mechanical, including
photocopying, recording, or any information storage and retrieval
system, without permission in writing from the publisher.

ISBN 1 85684 037-9

Unless otherwise stated, Scripture quotations in this publication are
from the Holy Bible, New International Version. Copyright © 1973,
1978, 1984 International Bible Society. Published in Great Britain by
Hodder & Stoughton Ltd.

Typeset by Saxon Graphics Ltd, Derby
Printed in Great Britain for Crossway Books, Norton Street,
Nottingham NG7 3HR by Cox & Wyman Ltd, Reading, Berkshire

Contents

Contents

Crossway Bible Guides

Series Editors' Introduction

Today, the groups of people who meet together to study the Bible appear to be a booming leisure-time activity in many parts of the world. In the United Kingdom alone, over one million people each week meet in home Bible-study groups.

This series has been designed to help such groups – and, in particular, those who lead them. We are also aware of the needs of those who preach and teach to larger groups as well as the hard-pressed student, all of whom often look for a commentary that gives a concise summary and lively application of a particular passage. We have tried to keep three clear aims in our sights:

1. To explain and apply the message of the Bible in non-technical language.
2. To encourage discussion, prayer and action on what the Bible teaches.
3. To enlist authors who are in the business of teaching the Bible to others and are doing it well.

All of us engaged in the project believe that the Bible is the Word of God – given to us in order that people might discover Him and His purposes for our lives. We believe that the 66 books which go to make up the Bible although written by different people, in different places, at different times, through different circumstances, have a single unifying theme: that theme is Salvation.

All of us hope that the books in this series will help people get a grip on the message of the Bible. But most important of all, we pray that the Bible will get a grip on you as a result!

Ian Coffey   Stephen Gaukroger
Series Editors

Note to readers

In our Bible Guides, we have developed special symbols, to make things easier to follow. Every passage therefore has an opening section which is:

the passage in a nutshell

The main section is the one that *makes sense of the passage.* This is marked with a blackboard.

Questions: Every passage also has special questions for group and personal study in a box after the main section. Some questions are addressed to us as individuals, some speak to us as members of our church or home group, while others concern us as members of God's people worldwide.

Some passages, however, require an extra amount of explanation, and we have put these sections into two categories. The first kind gives additional background material that help us understand something complex. For example, if we study the Gospels, it helps us to know who the Pharisees were, so that we can see more easily why they related to Jesus in the way they did. These technical sections are marked with an open book.

Finally, some passages have important doctrines contained in them, which we need to study in more depth if we are to grow as Christians. Special sections that explain them to us in greater detail are marked with a mortar board.

Acts 1:1–5

The Story Continues

The early Christians had all seen Jesus in the flesh, but they needed His power to do His work. 2,000 years later we still need this power.

Luke wrote his gospel and then turned his attention to writing a sequel – The Acts of the Apostles. Having told Theophilus ('Friend of God') all about the life of Jesus, he now wants to update him on all the exciting developments which have taken place since he wrote last. Theophilus was probably not a Christian but someone Luke knew, and who was fascinated by all he had heard about Jesus. He may have been a senior Roman official; Theophilus may even have been a code-name to disguise his true identity. What we do know is that, having whetted his appetite telling Theophilus about Jesus, he now goes on to tell him about the impact of His followers. Acts is their exciting story!

Luke is at pains to point out the link between volume I (Luke) and volume II (Acts). The link is Jesus. He does not just leave His disciples in the lurch, He gives clear instructions about what they are to do when He has gone. Not only that, but for over a month He keeps turning up just to reassure them. The resurrection is no 'flash-in the-pan' experience, a glimpse of Jesus in an unexpected moment; Jesus is alive! This is no phantom or figment of the imagination – the disciples see Him (verse 3), He teaches them (verse 2) and eats with them (verse 4). This is not 'normal' behaviour for a ghost or hallucination!

On top of all this Jesus makes sure that they are aware of the resources available to them. 'Don't go charging off into ministry before you are equipped' He says. He reminds them that John the Baptist knew that his baptism was only half the story (Mark 1:8). He sends them home to receive the best half!

So these anxious followers are meant to be reassured by the teaching of Jesus, the presence of Jesus and the power of Jesus. Christians at the end of the twentieth century have these same three resources available to them. Those first disciples faced losing their leader and friend. When we face 'loss', of whatever kind, we can draw strength from the teaching, presence and power of Jesus. We can receive these blessings through personal prayer, the support of a home group and in the regular services of the church.

Questions

1. *'Many convincing proofs' (verse 3). What evidence is there for the resurrection of Jesus?*

2. *Do I know the power of the Holy Spirit in my life? How can I experience Him?*

3. *Think of a lonely or sad person in your church. How can you help them draw on the resources which this passage describes?*

Background to Acts

The book of Acts seems to be the second part of a two volume work by Dr. Luke. The style, grammar and approach of both parts are very similar and the 'dedication' is to the same person – Theophilus (Luke 1:3 cf. Acts 1:1).

It was written over a number of months (or years?) becoming available to the church between A.D. 65 and 70. The story of Acts begins with the ascension (around A.D. 30) and covers the next thirty two years of early church history; ending with Paul spending two years under house arrest, until A.D. 62.

The first half of the book is dominated by Peter, the second half by Paul. With its 28 chapters and 1,007 verses, Acts is one of the longest books in the New Testament.

Introducing Luke

Luke appears three times in the New Testament. From these references we learn that he was a medical doctor and a close friend of Paul (Col. 4:14). Paul obviously saw Luke as an important part of his ministry team, a Christian worker as well as a friend (Philemon verse 24) and valued as a colleague who remained faithful even when others left (2 Tim. 4:11).

Luke was a Gentile Christian who seems to have been a well educated man, with a real heart for mission. Probably first called in when Paul needed medical help, he became much more than a personal physician – perhaps the first missionary doctor. His modesty is such that he avoids mentioning himself in either his Gospel or in Acts.

We have very few details about the life of Luke apart from the brief references already mentioned. There is some evidence to suggest that he died, aged 74, in the region to the south of the Black Sea. What we do know is that without him we would be almost totally ignorant about the early church and its mission.

Acts 1:6–11

Power to Tell Others

The disciples needed their focus to be changed and their lives to be renewed. This was a key to mission then – and it still is today.

The disciples were asking the wrong question. Jesus did not have a narrow nationalistic agenda. He was not about to boot out the Romans and establish His followers as the ruling government of the day. Some of His followers were still wanting positions of influence (Mark 10:35–41) in an earthly kingdom. Was this when Jesus was planning His coup? Even after all this time with Jesus they are still missing the point. He keeps explaining to them about the kingdom (verse 3), trying to get it into their heads that His kingdom is bigger than all their political, religious and cultural expectations. Their relatively small concerns would be handled by God the Father, in His own time and way. They were not to worry about the timetable.

Jesus tries to shift their focus back to the business of life in HIS kingdom. When the promised power (verse 5) arrives, they will be able to spread the news of this kingdom all over the world. In His typically direct manner, Jesus challenges and envisions in the same sentence. They are to tell their friends and family in the locality, but not be limited to this. They, and their fellow believers, will go all over the planet, telling what they know about Jesus and His kingdom.

Jesus then leaves them (verse 9). This remarkable scene ensures that these early followers did not think that Jesus just wandered off somewhere and died in obscurity. No, the miracle of the resurrection is followed by the miracle of the ascension. No doubt the disciples were completely mesmerised by this amazing sight and were glad of the angelic words of reassurance. 'Do not worry about staring into space, Jesus is in heaven and will come back to earth sometime in the future'. This message from the angels confirms the reality of heaven and the amazing truth that their friend and master is not finished with the earth. Another trip is planned!

This passage promises power for their missionary task. It reminds us – in the very last words of Jesus – what our focus as Christians is meant to be: telling the world about Jesus. Other concerns may be important, this concern is vital. These verses also remind us of where Jesus is now: with His Father in heaven. Heaven is also our final destination, and Jesus is one day coming back to take us to heaven with Him (John 14:1–4).

Questions

1. *In the light of this passage, do you think evangelism has a high enough priority in your church?*
2. *'... ends of the earth' (verse 8). Do you support an overseas missionary? How can you encourage your church to give more money/prayer to foreign mission?*
3. *Do you get excited about heaven? What are you most looking forward to?*

Resurrection

The resurrection of Jesus is a major emphasis in the book of Acts. Acts opens with an appearance of the risen Jesus (1:3–9) and the rest of the book is 'peppered' with references to His resurrection. Peter finds it difficult to preach a sermon without mentioning it (e.g. 2:24, 3:15) and Paul's preaching is similarly influenced by this fact!
(e.g. 13:30, 17:31, 26:23). For both men, the resurrection demonstrates the reliability of the messenger (Jesus) and the message (the gospel).

Peter and Paul follow this up in their letters, where they see the resurrection of Jesus as central to the Christian faith and its out-working in Christian discipleship (1 Cor. 15: 14, 1 Peter 1:3).

Acts does not present arguments in order to prove the resurrection, it simply accepts it as a fact. For those who had seen, touched and spoken with Jesus, the issue was beyond doubt!

Evangelism

The first Christians saw evangelism as a natural response
to their own conversion, based on a command from Jesus
(1:8 cf. Matt. 28:18–20). Only Philip is actually described
as an evangelist (21:8) and this is to distinguish him from
Philip the Apostle (1:13), rather than to indicate a formal
title.

Sharing the good news was seen as the responsibility and privilege of
everyone. Apostles evangelised (Peter and John), prophets evangelised
(Barnabas), teachers evangelised (Paul) and even deacons evangelised
(Stephen and Philip)! Telling others about Jesus seems to be a very high
priority; it is the focus of almost every chapter in Acts.

This is even more remarkable when you consider the pressure they were
under to be silent. Faced with this kind of opposition, most of us would be
content to let evangelism slip down our list of priorities.

Acts 1:12–14

Waiting for God to Act

The followers of Jesus obey Him by waiting for the power He promised. They wait together and in prayer. Obedience and prayer are still the characteristics of faithful Christians.

The disciples take the one kilometre journey back to base, in Jerusalem. It was a relatively short walk, though perhaps over rocky or steep terrain. It was a very long journey emotionally – back from the mountain-top experience of the ascension into the valley of city life. They congregate in an upper room (perhaps the room they had celebrated Passover in (Mark 14:12–16)) to assess the situation.

Luke then tells who was in this initial group. Basically, it is the original twelve (minus Judas Iscariot) and some of the women who so loyally supported Jesus throughout His life and even in His death (John 19:25). In addition to this group, Luke also mentions members of Jesus' family. This last group comes as something of a shock. The family of Jesus did not seem to be amongst His greatest supporters while He was alive, some of them even accusing Him of madness (Mark 3:21). Perhaps the death and resurrection of Jesus had caused them to think (and act) differently. Mary seems to have been the only family member to be consistently loyal toward her son.

These three groups form the nucleus of the group which was going to have such a profound impact in the ancient world. It is hard to imagine a less 'successful' bunch of people! Some frightened fishermen and the odd tax collector, supported by a few uneducated women with some only-recently-loyal family members thrown in. Not the best material for launching a new enterprise in a hostile world. Luke lists this unlikely crowd to emphasise that what follows in his book is not the product of human intellect and planning, but is the activity of the risen Jesus; operating by His Spirit. The 'Acts of the Apostles' is the title of the book, another title might be the 'Acts of the Holy Spirit'! There is no mere human explanation for what follows in Luke's story of the early church.

This section closes with a reference to two key principles of success for the first Christians: they were 'together' and 'in prayer' (verse 14). United prayer remains an incredibly potent force in any church. Many Christians (and their churches) often substitute activity for prayer, when God wants activity as a result of prayer and empowered by prayer. Prayer is the work of the church. It should never be an excuse for idleness or avoiding costly action, but it must precede, accompany and follow all our activity as the people of God.

Questions

1. *Are you surprised by the kind of people God chose to start his Church? What kind of people would you have chosen?*

2. *How committed have you been to corporate prayer in your Church? In what ways could you be more involved in the prayer life of your local fellowship?*

3. *'All joined together' (verse 14). How can you encourage unity in your house group? Church? Home?*

Acts 1:15–26

Replacing a Leader

Judas has gone and his place in the apostolic team needs to be filled. A replacement is wisely and prayerfully chosen.

Peter, always a man of action, begins a speech designed to encourage the early Christians to choose a successor to Judas Iscariot. It seems that in the days and weeks after the ascension, the upper room became a regular meeting place for the committed believers: 120 of them. Peter is emerging as one of the key leaders and immediately points the group back to Scripture as their authority and guide. Judas, whose name is mentioned with anger and disappointment, comes to a gruesome end. He is a traitor, both to Jesus personally and to the first century believers generally. With the 'blood money' he is given by the Jewish leaders he buys a field in which his own blood is spilled. Peter seems to imply that he gets what he deserves!

If Judas is to be replaced (and Peter quotes Psalm 69:25 and Psalm 109:8 to show he ought to be) then they need to establish the personal qualifications required for such a significant task. Peter summarises the main qualification as being part of the group since Jesus began His ministry – a period of about three years. Their central task would be to act as a witness to the truth of the resurrection. Two candidates emerge. After prayer, they 'cast lots' to see which candidate is successful. Matthias is chosen. In Jewish history (and throughout the ancient world) the throwing of various objects on the ground – dice, stones, bones, etc. – was a common way of discovering the will of God. However, this was no mere superstition or reliance on 'fate'. Proverbs 16:33 shows that they believed God was the one who ultimately decided what happened.

This passage identifies three steps in the process of leader selection: an assessment of personal qualification, commitment of the issue to God in prayer, and allowing God to make the appointment. The first two steps must be undertaken with care and seriousness. There are no short cuts to getting these things right. Individuals who are potential leaders must have their relationship with Jesus examined and every member of the church family must commit the matter to God in prayer. *How* the leader is appointed will vary from church to church (for example by vote; appointment by other leaders; unanimous affirmation?, etc.) depending on our denominational practice or cultural background. Whatever the mechanism for the decision, it must allow God's will to be revealed and acted on.

Questions

1. *Why doesn't everyone who 'betrays' God end up like Judas – dead and discredited (verse 18)?*

2. *In what ways do we behave like traitors to Jesus or our fellow Christians?*

3. *How does your church appoint its leaders? Is it a better or worse system than casting lots (verse 26)? Why?*

Leadership

Acts sees the first leaders of the early church as the apostles. Because Judas is dead, a replacement is needed to keep the leadership team up to strength (1:20–26). Peter soon emerges as the dominant personality, although the 'chairman' of the apostolic team seems to be James (15:13, 21:18).

As time goes by elders are appointed (14:23, 15:22) with responsibility for spiritual oversight for a particular local church (cf. 20:17). Deacons are appointed in Jerusalem (6:1–6) and eventually more widely in the local church (cf. Phil. 1:1). Their role appears to be more specific than the elders, though not necessarily lower in status. Both groups have high qualification guidelines (1 Tim. 3:8–13, Titus 1:5–9) but little is known about their method of appointment or the exact outworking of their function.

The two other leadership roles appear to be prophet and teacher (13:1, 21:10, cf. Eph. 4:11). These roles – apostle, prophet, elder, deacon, teacher – do not appear to be completely separate ministries; some people seem to exercise more than one role or even a mixture of roles. In Acts, the emphasis is not on a definitive description of leadership role or status, but on a statement about gifting and ministry to support a growing church. For the New Testament as a whole, function and action (not position or structure) are the important facets of leadership.

Acts 2:1–13

The Holy Spirit is Released

After waiting for Jesus to fulfil His promise, all heaven breaks loose among the 120. They speak in tongues and amaze the city. God is still pouring out His Spirit on the Church.

Pentecost was a well established Jewish feast. It means 'fiftieth' and was a celebration of the grain harvest. Pentecost happened on the fiftieth day after Passover, when seven weeks' worth of harvest had been gathered in. It was also the occasion of the anniversary of the Law being given on Sinai. The significance of this would not have been lost on the first Christians – the old covenant had been characterised by the operation of the laws, the new covenant would be characterised by the operation of the Spirit. With a marvellous sense of divine timing the new era is ushered in on the anniversary of the old as they meet together.

Luke describes what happens next as best he can, considering the incredible event he was witnessing. A noise like a tornado blowing through the room, a roaring fire that appeared from nowhere, then separated into individual flames on a hundred and twenty heads, followed by the expression of lots of different languages being spoken out in wonder and amazement! A scene of godly disorder and holy disarray.

Because it was the feast of Pentecost thousands of Jews found themselves in Jerusalem. They were obviously outside in the street when they heard the commotion among the disciples. Perhaps the noise (followed by the disciples!) burst out of the upper room, developed into a meeting on the streets and ended up as a huge gathering somewhere in the temple precincts. We cannot be sure about the details but we can be certain about the impact on the hearers! They seem to have come from all over the known world and yet they all heard the disciples praising God in their own languages. Even when faced with this amazing miracle, some of the crowd thought the whole affair owed its origin to a totally different kind of spirit (verse 13).

It's important to notice in this passage that, despite the amazing physical signs (noise, fire, tongues) Luke emphasises the spiritual cause – they 'were filled with the Holy Spirit' (verse 4). Pentecost is the birth-day of the Church. The start of the ministry of Jesus was affirmed by the Spirit (Matt. 3:16) so it is appropriate for the start of the Church to be affirmed by the same Spirit.

Questions

1. *What do you think it must have felt like to be in Jerusalem on that particular Pentecost? Do you think you would have recognised God at work in all the noise or would you have been on the side of the cynics (verse 13)?*

2. *What do you feel about 'speaking in tongues'? Try and put yourself in the position of a Christian who does not speak in tongues (if you do) or who does (if you don't)! How do you feel? (e.g. superior? confident? not bothered?)*

3. *Why do you think Luke goes to all the trouble of listing so many places by name? Is it significant that 'Arabs' get a mention (verse 11)?*

The Gift of Tongues

The reference in 2:4 to speaking in tongues is the first reference to the phenomenon in Acts. 'Tongues' appears at various points in Luke's account as a sign of the presence of the Holy Spirit (cf. 10:46, 19:6). Luke views it as a common external evidence of the Holy Spirit's activity, but not as an essential manifestation of the filling with the Spirit (e.g. its absence from Paul's conversion story (9:17–19).

These 'tongues' were human languages on the day of Pentecost, but they appear to be mainly angelic languages in the rest of Acts and the later Letters (e.g. 1 Cor. 13:1). Paul expresses gratitude for the fact that he has this gift (1 Cor. 14:18) and lays down guidelines for its public use (1 Cor. 14:5–25).

Paul is critical of the way 'tongues' was used at Corinth, not negative about the gift itself. The Bible seems to give little support to those who wish to consign this gift to history, and similarly little to those who wish to elevate it to an essential requirement of the Spirit-filled life!

Acts 2:14–21

A Challenging Sermon – Part I

This part of the sermon is an attempt to explain what the crowd have just seen and heard. It describes Pentecost as God keeping His promise to the Jews – a faithful God.

The coming of the Holy Spirit in such a dramatic way certainly got people's attention! Peter is not slow to seize the opportunity to speak to the crowd, trying to explain what has happened. We ought to note the remarkable change in Peter since he denied Jesus (Luke 22:54–61). His restoration by Jesus (John 21:15–22) has transformed him. We can thank God that He does not wash His hands of us when we fail! It's such a large crowd that Peter has to shout (no P.A. system) to be heard, and is quick to point out how early in the morning it is. Their behaviour is not the result of alcoholic excess but the fulfilment of Joel 2:28–32.

The Jews were looking for the day when Messiah would come ('the last days', verse 17) bringing with Him great signs of power. This new era would be characterised by God's Spirit being released on men and women, young and old ... with prophecies, dreams and visions being the order of the day. How different this was from the old era, when only specially chosen individuals had access to the Spirit's power. Now He is available to 'all people' (verse 17). 'God told Joel about this, Joel passed it on, and what you see here today is simply God doing what He said He would', Peter informs the astonished gathering.

The details of Joel's prophecy are of little interest to Peter. He does not stop to explain about the blood and fire (verse 19) or the moon turning to blood (verse 20). These things may have happened on the afternoon of the crucifixion (cf. Luke 23:44,45), they may be symbolic or perhaps they will occur when the Messiah who has just left (1:11) comes back to judge the world (Rev. 6:12). We cannot be certain about these issues and anyway we ought to emphasise the general thrust of the passage as Peter does.

The central message is that God is faithful to what He promises; the Holy Spirit has been released just as Joel prophesied. The new era has begun! And this new era is open to 'everyone who calls on the name of the Lord' (verse 21). What an amazing offer! And this 'special offer' has never been withdrawn; we can take advantage of it at the end of the twentieth century just as they did at the start of the first century.

Questions

1. *It was a long time between Joel's prophecy and its fulfilment at Pentecost! Why do we find it so difficult to be patient, waiting for God to act?*

2. *Do you think prophecy, visions and dreams have a place in church life today? What are the strengths/dangers of these things?*

3. *What does 'be saved' (verse 21) mean? 'Saved' from what? To what? How?*

Prophecy

Prophets in the New Testament had a ministry (inspired by the Spirit) of foretelling future events (11:28, 21:10,11) and of building up the people of God (15:32, 1 Cor. 14:3). Sometimes they had a travelling ministry (11:27) and on other occasions seem to be attached to a specific local situation (e.g. Antioch (13:1)).

The *gift* of prophecy could also be exercised by those who were not necessarily called to the *ministry* of the prophet (e.g. 2:17,18; 19:6); so 'ordinary' Christians could use this gift to build up the church. Paul values the gift very highly indeed (1 Cor. 14:5) and encourages its use in the Church (1 Cor. 14:1).

Acts 2:22–28

A Challenging Sermon – Part II

Peter continues his message by focusing on Jesus – particularly His cruel death – and showing Him as God's agent, bringing in the new era.

This part of the sermon emphasises the humanity of Jesus. The word 'man' is used twice in the opening verses and He is identified as coming from a town many of them would know – about sixty miles north of Jerusalem. But even the crowd knew He was not an ordinary man (verse 22). Some would have eaten with the five thousand (Luke 9:10-17), seen the sick healed (Mark 1:32–34) or heard the amazing reports about Lazarus (John 11:38–48). Despite all this, the crowd were guilty of hounding this extraordinary man to His death; a brutal death by Roman execution. God's hand was in all this to work out His purposes, but that did not excuse their awful behaviour. They killed God's messenger!

Peter, who has only just realised this himself (John 20:3–9), describes the death of Jesus like the birth pains before birth. Agonising and painful, but resulting in life not death. Yet again he quotes the Old Testament (Psalm 16:8–11) to demonstrate that God is doing what He said He would. By calling David as a witness for the prosecution, Peter cites one of the great heroes of the Jewish faith. If anyone can convince them of the error of their ways, and the truth of what Peter is saying, surely David can! They are guilty as charged.

In his Psalm David points, prophetically, to God's care of His Son – He would not be 'abandoned' (verse 27a). Of course, Jesus felt abandoned and utterly alone (Psalm 22:1 cf. Matt. 27:46) but after three days was wonderfully raised to life. God was faithful to His word, despite what seemed like a lot of evidence to the contrary. Because of the embalming process (John 19:39–40), His body did not even begin to decay over those three days (verse 27b). What was written hundreds of years earlier (about 980 B.C.?) was fulfilled in Jesus!

These verses point us to Jesus, the focal point of God's purpose and plan. As we look to Jesus, and the way the Father was faithful to Him, we can draw strength for ourselves. Many of us have periods in our lives when we feel terribly alone, abandoned by God to fend for ourselves. We may have been abused, bereaved or rejected. Whatever our feelings, we can be sure about God's faithfulness. He did not forsake His Son, He will not forsake His sons and daughters.

Questions

1. *So far in the book of Acts, Peter has quoted the Old Testament four times. Could you have done this?! Why is the Old Testament neglected by so many Christians?*

2. *If Jesus turned up in your town doing miracles (verse 22) how do you think people would respond?*

3. *Which groups of people in the world might think that God has abandoned them? How can we help them?*

Acts 2:29–36

A Challenging Sermon – Part III

The sermon ends with a declaration of the divinity of Jesus, affirmed by His resurrection from the dead. There is no-one quite like this Jesus!

Peter, by now rising to a crescendo of passion in preaching, points out the obvious. David is dead. So Psalm 16 cannot be about him, it must be about somebody else. And as David has not 'ascended' into heaven, Psalm 110:1 (cf. verses 34,35) can't be about him either. Jesus had already implied that this Psalm was about Himself (Mark 12:35–37) and Peter builds on this understanding. Notice again the emphasis on the reliability and faithfulness of God: He 'promised him on oath' (verse 30) and God was as good as His word.

The resurrection of Jesus is the central fact of this sermon; everything else hangs on this truth. Peter is at pains to point out that he is not guessing about this or going on rumour or second-hand reports. He saw Jesus alive from the dead with his own eyes (1 Cor. 15:5) and so had these other disciples standing with him (1:3 cf. verse 32, 1 Cor. 15:6). There is no doubt about it. Peter's implication is that this fact is beyond dispute. They (like us!) could debate, procrastinate or even deny it, but nothing would change the truth.

What must have really shocked this already 'amazed' (verse 7) congregation was what Peter said about the alive Jesus. Firstly, he told them that Jesus was none other than the Messiah they had been looking for – the Christ (verses 31,36). The Messiah (Christ is the Greek word for Messiah: 'The anointed one') was Jesus. They need look for Him no longer.

Secondly, Jesus was the Lord (verses 34,36). Old Testament references to God are taken as applying to Jesus; Peter is putting Jesus on the same level as God Himself! This revelation must have been staggering to the gathered Jewish crowd. All the honour, adoration and worship which they have reserved for God alone, was also due to a poor carpenter from Nazareth.

The early disciples were clear about who Jesus was. They would have found many of our explanations of Jesus quite funny, in a tragic sort of way. 'Just a good man', 'a wise teacher', 'an example of love and kindness' ... all these accolades fall far short of Peter's clear, full-blooded, uncompromising description of the One who ushered in God's kingdom (1:3). He is the 'anointed one', fully God and fully man. The defeater of death and the baptiser with the Holy Spirit!

Questions

1. *None of us saw the resurrection of Jesus with our own eyes (see verse 32). In what ways can we testify that it is true? (In our experience? Intellectually?)*

2. *'Jesus was just a good man'. What reasons would you give for disagreeing with this statement?*

3. *Peter really emphasises the resurrection. Why do you think it is such an important part of Christian faith? What would happen to Christianity if it wasn't true (see 1 Cor. 15:14)?*

Acts 2:37–47

The Growing Church

There is an amazing response to Peter's sermon and the church begins to get established. Being a Christian soon affects every part of their lives.

Many in the crowd were convicted by the thought that they had contributed to the death of God's Messiah. Their spirits were in great distress ('cut to the heart') as they pleaded with Peter about what to do. Peter immediately offers a two-step solution: repentance (a complete change of mind, turning around and going the other way!) and baptism, acknowledging that Jesus really is God's Anointed One. When they do this all their evil will be forgiven and they too will receive the blessing of the new era – the Holy Spirit. And the offer is not restricted to them but available to family and friends, even to those who lived many miles away from Jerusalem.

Three thousand people responded to this offer immediately (the original 'upper room' group is increased twenty five times over, in one day!) and joined themselves to the believers. This led to the rapid introduction of a Discipleship Course, which covered such foundational subjects as Christian Doctrine, Fellowship, Communion and Prayer (verse 42). Just as in the first century, it is a vitally important part of church life to provide for the nurture and care of new converts.

The passage goes on to describe life in the early church. The church was characterised by signs of supernatural power (verse 43), prolonged fellowship (verse 44), generous and sacrificial giving (verse 45), eating and praising God (verses 46,47) and meeting on a daily basis (verse 46), no doubt for worship and teaching. As the early Christians multiplied and spread out over the ancient world, some of the details in this pattern changed, but the principles were retained. It was not Luke's intention to imply, for example, that Christians must meet together every day, as they did here; but it is obviously his intention to highlight the value of regular gatherings for prayer, fellowship and worship. (Churches must be very careful as they apply this passage to congregational life. We may feel justified in reducing 'everything in common' (verse 44) to 'sharing a few things' and 'selling their possessions'.(verse 45) to 'trying to be generous'; but we ought to note that we have also managed to reduce 'wonders and miraculous signs' (verse 43) to 'no-one was converted but God really blessed us'!

Such was the power of God on these believers that *every day* (verse 47) new people were joining the worshipping community. What a thrill to be part of a church like this!

Questions

1. *What signs are there in a person's life when repentance is real (verse 38)?*

2. *What do we need to do to make sure new Christians keep growing and are kept from drifting away?*

3. *Why do we find sharing our possessions so difficult? What do you think a first century Christian would think of the way we treat the things we own?*

Prayer

Prayer was a vital part of the life of the early church. It was a significant part of their spiritual lives together (2:42) and a major part of the apostles' role (6:4) as leaders in the Christian community. They prayed for protection and boldness (4:24–30), when ordaining elders, deacons and missionaries (18:23, 6:6, 13:3), when wanting to help people receive the Holy Spirit (8:15) and as a regular exercise of corporate worship (3:1, 16:13).

They offered prayers of praise (4:24), thanksgiving (27:35) and desperation (12:5)! They saw prayer as part and parcel of their corporate walk with

God. There is very little emphasis on personal prayer in Acts. A fleeting reference to Peter (10:9) and Paul (9:11) praying privately is the only mention it gets! Praying with other Christians is highlighted as the mechanism God uses to reveal His will, release His blessing and accomplish His purposes.

Acts 3:1–10

The First Healing

God acts in power to confirm the ministry of the apostles and the authority of His Son. It is a miracle motivated by compassion.

Peter and John were going to pray, along with other Jews, at the temple. This was the second of three prayer opportunities each day (early morning, mid-afternoon and sunset) which the Jews observed. They see a chronically disabled beggar on his way to the temple, not to pray but to beg. This was not an unusual sight in ancient Jerusalem; Peter and John must have passed dozens of pathetic characters on their journey to prayer. For some reason they are drawn to this particular beggar and they lead him to believe that he is in for a sizable donation ('look at us', verses 4,5). His hopes are dashed as Peter tells the man of his own poverty. (Presumably he had given it all away (2:45)). His hopes are revived by a mind-blowing statement which draws on the power of Jesus and results in a clear command – 'walk' (verse 6).

It is important to note that Peter is not responsible for the healing – Jesus is. Peter is the agent God uses (and his courage in making this statement ought to be applauded) but the power for the healing comes from the Anointed One; better known to the people in Jerusalem as Jesus from Nazareth.

The beggar cannot believe his ears and needs Peter to offer the 'right hand of fellowship' (verse 7) to encourage him to his feet. He is completely and instantaneously healed! And this is a man who has never, ever walked before. He was born with a body deformed in some way (verse 2), giving him a 'permanent' disability. No wonder he cannot keep still. He leaps and jumps and walks ... and all the time is praising God (verse 8). The temple courts had never seen anything like it. People were 'filled with wonder' (verse 10) at this man they may just have given some money to as a disabled beggar, now rushing about all over the place celebrating his healing by worshipping God.

It is particularly thrilling that the first miracle of the early church recorded in detail, should be such a difficult one. You might have expected the apostles to start by trying to heal someone with a cold, a sprained ankle or a small boil! No, straight in at the deep end, a man crippled from birth. Nothing is too difficult for Jesus. As Peter and John discovered, the 'impossible' is possible for Him.

Questions

1. Does the 'Name of Jesus' (verse 6b) still have the same power to heal today? In what ways should we encourage this?

2. Peter and John had no money (verse 6a) but they were used to heal this sick man. Do you think there is a connection between these two? (i.e. poverty and power).

3. This miracle is both quick and complete. Why do you think that healing like this is so rare today?

Miracles

There are at least eighteen specific supernatural events recorded in Acts and another ten occasions where there is a general reference to miracles occurring. (This is an average of one reference for each of the 28 chapters in Acts!) It is impossible to remove them from the story without destroying the account completely. Luke does not record these miracles with exaggeration or dwell on them excessively; they simply form one part of the life of the early church, so he reports them accurately and concisely.

It is hardly surprising that a God who can raise Jesus from the dead is capable of other (easier?) miracles. These supernatural events seem to occur most when the gospel is proclaimed for the first time in a particular location or to a particular group. They seem to be 'performed' mainly by the leadership of the church. In combination with teaching (cf. 13:9–12), they result in thousands discovering Jesus.

Acts 3:11–16

Another Powerful Sermon

Peter takes the opportunity of the healing miracle to preach an evangelistic message! This first part of the sermon points to Jesus and the power of faith.

This healed beggar will not let Peter and John out of his sight. Perhaps he thinks once they go, his healing would also go. (An understandable fear, but he is mistaken). He 'held on to' (verse 11) the apostles – it is the same phrase used to describe an arrest by the police! – clinging to them while the crowd grows around the unlikely trio. Fortu-

nately, Solomon's colonnade was large, running the entire length of the eastern end of the temple. Once the crowd assemble, Peter, never one to miss an opportunity, preaches a sermon of explanation. It has a number of the same elements as the Pentecost sermon: the opening style (verse 12 cf. 2:22), an accusation about killing Jesus (verses 13–15a cf. 2:23), the exaltation by God of Jesus (verse 13 cf. 2:36) and Peter's own credentials as a witness of the resurrection (verse 15 cf. 2:32).

If anything, this sermon is even more passionate in tone than the Pentecost sermon. Verses 13b-15a contain a damning indictment of the Jews; a blunt, accusatory attack on their role in the death of Jesus. Peter makes no attempt to soften these savage verbal blows – this is no-nonsense preaching at its most direct. We have much to learn from this. Gentleness and discretion are important facets of the preacher's skill, but this must never be allowed to blunt the cutting edge of the message. We are often far too afraid of causing offence or upsetting people with a raw, unpackaged presentation of gospel truth. We must pray for a holy boldness.

Peter is at pains to refuse all credit for the miracle (verse 12) and points to a divine aspect and a human aspect in the cure. It is the name of Jesus which has power (verse 16 cf. 2:38) and the power is seen in response to faith. (In this case it is the faith of Peter and John, not the faith of the crippled man). And there is no possibility of a hoax; they had all passed this man, in his disabled condition, day after day as he sat begging at the ornate gateway into the temple area. The crowd themselves were the best evidence for this miracle (verse 16)! There is no escape from the truth about the person of Jesus, nor from the fact of the healing miracle. God has been at work.

Questions

1. How many titles or descriptions of God's Son can you find in this passage? Why does Peter use so many?
2. If we do not see healing miracles like this, is it because we lack faith (verse 16)? Or are there other reasons?
3. The passage talks of disowning Jesus twice (verses 13,14). In what circumstances are you tempted to disown Jesus? Why?

Acts 3:17–26

Jesus – Fulfilling the Scripture

Peter's sermon continues by demonstrating how Jesus is God's long-promised Christ; he calls for repentance. The same call is appropriate today.

The sermon continues in these verses, but in more restrained style. They represent the 'carrot' approach, the 'stick' having been effectively used in verses 13–15. Peter addresses them as 'brothers' and concedes that they may not have been completely aware of the implications of what they were doing when they killed Jesus. Ignorance is no excuse (cf. Lev. 5:17) but it does in some measure lessen their guilt. God had it in mind all along to use the suffering of Christ to accomplish His purposes (verse 18 cf. 2:23).

These verses pose a problem for us, in a way that would not have worried the first hearers. We find it hard to reconcile the fact that the death of Jesus was part of God's plan, with the fact that He was killed by evil men. How could they be blamed for doing what God had decided to do anyway? The Jews had an understanding of God which allowed Him total authority, while giving His creatures the dignity of making meaningful decisions. We are not puppets, being made to respond every time our strings are pulled. The Scripture affirms both truths equally – sinful human beings (verse 15) and the plan of God (verse 18) put Jesus on the cross.

Peter then points the crowd back to their Old Testament Scriptures. These Scriptures have been paving the way for all that they have witnessed in recent weeks. Moses (verse 22), Samuel (verse 24), Abraham (verse 25) and 'all the prophets' (verse 24) are quoted as 'signposts' which pointed forward to Jesus. 'These great Jewish leaders foretold the coming of the Messiah and you are immensely privileged, because He has come to you first', Peter told them (verse 26).

Repentance is the key (verse 19 cf. 2:38) to unlocking the blessing of the Christ. If they repent there will be implications for the past and the present, continuing on into the future. God will take His sponge and clean out all the dirt from your cuts and wounds ('sins may be wiped out') and into the barren deserts of your lives His presence will come like showers of rain on an oppressively hot day ('Times of refreshing'). Repentance is still the key to unlocking the blessings of God. Without genuine repentance we will not experience all that God has for us. The powerlessness of some church-goers is directly related to the absence of genuine repentance.

Questions
1. *In what ways is repentance more than simply 'being sorry'?*
2. *How can we keep our Christian life 'refreshed' (verse 19)? How can we encourage other Christians to do the same?*
3. *Jesus came to the Jews 'first' (verse 26). Do we have a responsibility to continue to evangelise the Jews? Why have Jews and Christians had a history of distrust?*

Becoming a Christian

The book of Acts records several incidents where individuals become Christians (e.g. Saul, Cornelius, Lydia, Philippian Jailor) and on numerous occasions records large numbers of people responding to the Good News (e.g. 2:41, 4:4, 14:1, 17:4). We also have excerpts from sermons which call for people to respond to Christ. These three pieces of evidence combine to show us what Luke (and the early church) thought was involved in becoming a follower of Jesus.

There seem to be four aspects to the initial phase of following Jesus.
1. Repentance – a complete turning around and returning to God (2:38, 26:20).
2. Belief/faith – putting trust in the name and power of Jesus (16:31, 20:21).

3. Baptism in water (8:38, 9:18, 16:15).
4. The Holy Spirit's power (9:17, 10:44, 19:5).

Sometimes, one or more of these aspects is implied rather than clearly stated; and the order in which they occur varies from case to case. Nevertheless, Luke clearly sees these four things as vital components of the conversion experience. Today we are in danger of emphasising some of these things to the near-exclusion of one or more of the others. It is no wonder so many Christians do not get the best start to their lives as believers!

Acts 4:1–12

Peter and John on Trial

The apostles are arrested, imprisoned and tried. They speak in their own defence, by telling the court about the power of Jesus.

Before Peter's sermon can come to a proper conclusion, the chief of security at the temple arrives to see what all the fuss is about. The Sadducees (verse 1) were wealthy aristocrats who had maintained their status and affluence by collaborating with the Roman authorities. A disturbance in the temple is the last thing they need if

relationships with the Romans are to be kept sweet. Not only that, Peter's message is all about resurrection which they did not believe in: all in all, two good reasons for hushing the whole thing up and having the apostles thrown in prison (verse 3).

Jesus had warned His disciples to expect persecution (Luke 21:12); perhaps they had not thought it would come quite this quickly! However, despite the apostles being hauled away in mid-sentence, many people were convinced and joined the church. There are now over forty times as many believers as there were on the day of Pentecost (1:15 cf. verse 4)!

The Jewish council is convened (verse 5), with Luke at pains to point out that the top people are there (verse 6) – this is obviously a serious matter. They demand to know what is going on. Peter, pentecostally empowered, speaks for both the apostles when he gives a robust defence of their actions. (Jesus had promised they would have special power in situations like this (Luke 12:11,12) and so it proved!)

Peter makes the point that they ought to be pleased that a sick man is

41

now well – after all, it was an 'act of kindness' (verse 9). They had not healed the crippled man, Jesus had. The Jewish rulers were guilty of doing away with the Christ, in fulfilment of Psalm 118:22 (verses 10,11). If they wanted to be forgiven for this sin in particular and other sins in general, they could find salvation in Jesus and nowhere else. This is not a speech designed to win friends!

Verse 12 is the clearest statement so far in Acts of the uniqueness of Jesus. It has been implied by the disciples (John 6:68) and stated by Jesus (John 14:6). Now it appears in the teaching and experience of the early Church. It carries with it a blunt denial of the ability of the Jewish law (or any Roman or Greek deity that was popular at the time) to effect salvation. In a world of many faiths and religious viewpoints, Christianity continues to need this emphasis. Humbly communicated, it can energise our evangelism and enrich our worship.

Questions

1. *'All religions lead to God'. How does verse 12 affect our response to this?*

2. *Very few of us have been imprisoned for our faith. How can we support those who are persecuted for their faith around the world?*

3. *How many 'acts of kindness' (verse 9) have you done today? How can your house group/church develop a practical ministry of 'kindness'?*

Sanhedrin

The Sanhedrin was the highest authority in Jewish affairs. It was patterned on the court of Moses (cf. Num. 11:16,17) and had 70 members and a presiding chairman who co-ordinated its activities. Membership was only possible for Jewish married men who were over 30 years old.

There were three groups represented on the Sanhedrin: 'Rulers' – chief priests and priests with an official role or status in the synagogue; 'Elders' – those in lay-leadership, often drawn from wealthy aristocratic families; 'Scribes' – legal experts, often Pharisees. Together, this group formed the supreme council among the Jews. It had enjoyed a good reputation, but by the time of Jesus was dominated by self-serving 'politicians', not the godly men originally in mind when the council was formed. The New Testament views it almost always in a negative light – threatened by Jesus' ministry (John 11:47–53), engineering His death (Matt. 26:59) and attempting to bully His church into silence (Acts 5:21–40)!

Sadducees

The Sadducees were a political group with considerable influence at the time of Jesus and the early church. They were not a large group numerically (many fewer than the Pharisees) but made up of wealthy, influential individuals. They were very close to the Roman administration, often collaborating with the occupying power. They were not above bribery (or threats) to maintain their positions of power.

They did not believe in the resurrection, and on this point found themselves opposed by both the Pharisees and the Christians (Acts 23:6–8). Two of the three groups on the Sanhedrin (elders and rulers) would tend to support the Sadducees party.

Pharisees

The Pharisees were a large group of men who were characterised by their commitment to the customs and traditions of Judaism. They often had legal training and were sticklers for obedience to every single part of Jewish law. During the ministry of Jesus, they regularly opposed Him and His message (e.g. Luke 5:21,30); Jesus reserved some of His strongest language for this group (e.g. Luke 11:39f)!

By the time of the early church, however, their stance against the Christians had softened. The Pharisee, Gamaliel, comes to the Christians' rescue (Acts 5:34), they side with the Christians (against the Sadducees) about 'resurrection' (Acts 23:8) and some of their number even become Christians (Acts 15:5). Their most famous convert is the Apostle Paul! (Acts 23:6).

Acts 4:13–22

Warned, but Set Free

The trial ends with the apostles being released but warned about future behaviour. Their faith is undiminished by the Sanhedrin's threats.

The Jewish ruling council is amazed by the boldness of the fishermen (verse 13). By background they are the opposite of those who make up the Council. Peter and John had no professional or academic qualifications and yet could articulate their views with amazing clarity. Jesus had obviously taught them well (verse 13b).

The Council found itself in a difficult position. The man was obviously healed (after over 40 years of disability) and his presence at the trial (verse 14) made dismissing this evidence difficult. The crowd was delighted at God's healing power (verse 21b), everyone in the city was aware of the incredible thing Peter and John had done the day before (verse 16) and hundreds had decided to follow Jesus (verse 4). The Sanhedrin could only threaten them with punishment in the future if they kept on talking about Jesus. They were desperate for 'peace at any price'. Civic disturbances would attract the attention of the Roman authorities and put at risk their positions of power and influence.

The apostles and the Sanhedrin behave in ways which act as an example – one positive, the other negative! What matters to God is not our academic or intellectual ability but our openness to Him. Peter and John should have been 'taken to the cleaners' by the professors on the Sanhedrin. This would not be the last time God would demonstrate His power through the underdog! (1 Cor. 1:26–31). And notice how the Sanhedrin (all religious leaders) do not even address the issue of whether or not what Peter says is *true*; their minds are closed. Protecting their vested interests is all that concerns them. May God give us the courage always to be open to the truth – even if it challenges our lifestyle and behaviour.

Peter and John refuse to be cowed into silence. 'Make your own mind up', they say, 'should we obey you or God?' (verse 19). This is not rebellion against authority for its own sake, but rather the only possible response to an edict which was directly opposed to what Jesus had told them to do (Matt. 28:18–20 and 1:8). Not only that, they just cannot help themselves! The sight of the risen Jesus and all He taught them, just can't be kept quiet. They *have* to let the Good News out.

Questions

1. *Why are we so frightened about what people will think of us or say about us? How can we overcome this (see verse 20)?*

2. *Do you need a degree or professional qualification to be a leader in your church? What qualifications are important for leaders (e.g. look at verses 8, 13b, 19)?*

3. *Is our definition of a good sermon, 'one we agree with'? Why is this dangerous? What are the characteristics of a closed mind?*

Persecution

Luke tells an exciting story of life and growth as he describes the early church. But it is also a story of pain, pressure and persecution. The success of the first Christians was not without considerable cost.

They had recently lost their leader (1:9) and were soon being imprisoned (4:3), threatened (4:21), imprisoned again (5:18) and cruelly flogged (5:40). Stephen was stoned by a lynch-mob (7:57,58), James, the brother of John, was beheaded (12:2) and Paul was (amongst other things!) stoned (14:19), severely beaten (16:22,23), imprisoned (16:24) ... and shipwrecked (27:39–44)!

Let no-one doubt the incredible cost of Christian discipleship. These first-century believers certainly paid the price for their allegiance to Jesus. We may envy the success recorded in Acts, but we often forget the sacrifice that accompanied it!

45

Acts 4:23–31

The Praying Church

Peter and John join their friends for prayer. Worship and intercession lead to a fresh touch from God, which results in ever bolder evangelism.

After the council releases them, the dynamic duo report back to their fellow believers. As they recount the incident, the early church feels two conflicting emotions: joy because of the healing miracle and frustration (with a little fear) at the response of the Sanhedrin. These two responses dictate the shape of their prayer – Praise and Thanksgiving (verses 24–28), followed by Petition (verses 29,30).

Notice that prayer is their first response to the crisis (an example we would do well to emulate!) and it is a prayer that has God as its focus from the start. When in doubt, start by reminding yourself how great God is. This prayer talks of His supreme status as ruler over all He has created (verse 24). Psalm 2 is then quoted as a reminder of the futility of trying to thwart God's purposes (verses 25,26), then the prayer goes on to affirm the controlling hand of God over all that has happened (verse 28). The message of the first part of the prayer is – God is in charge. When trouble comes into our lives we would do well to remind ourselves of these characteristics of our God. They are designed to bring comfort and reassurance, just as they did here in the first century.

The prayer continues (verse 29) with a request for three things. (They weren't: l. Get the Sanhedrin off our backs. 2. Give us an alternative strategy. 3. Please grant us a quiet life. These prayers would certainly feature in many of our churches if we were faced with this situation!) They asked for: 1. God to take note of who His enemies were ('consider their threats'), 2. An increased boldness in speaking the word (verse 29b) and 3. Evidence of the supernatural (verse 30).

God was well aware of the trouble the religious leaders would cause the early church; His Son had not found them helpful, neither would His followers (Matt. 10:17, 24; 16:12; 26:59). The other two requests were answered in a spectacular and decisive fashion. The place where they were meeting was shaken (a divinely timed earthquake?) and the following days saw their courage increase (verse 31).

Luke tells that they were again filled with the Holy Spirit (verse 31). The outward signs are different from the filling they received at Pentecost (2:2–4), but the experience is no less real. We should look for signs of God's Spirit in those who claim to be filled with Him; but the nature of the sign must not absorb our attention, distracting us from the necessity of the filling!

Questions

1. Have you been filled with the Spirit (verse 31)? How do you know?

2. Why is prayer sometimes the last thing we do in a crisis, rather than the first? Who is going through a crisis in your church, whom you could pray for this week?

3. List some governments or organisations which 'threaten' the church. How can we help overcome them and support those Christians who are most at risk?

Acts 4:32-37

The Sharing Church

The Good News affected every area of the lives of the first Christians – even their money and possessions. This resulted in practical acts of compassion.

There is no doubt that the early church saw the sharing of possessions as a significant expression of their faith (verse 32b cf. 2:44). Luke believes these expressions of social concern are the outworking of the spiritual reality of the filling with the Holy Spirit. Just as tongues (2:4) and boldness (verse 31) are 'natural' results of the Spirit's activity, so Luke infers that loving, selfless sharing is another cháracteristic of the Spirit-filled life. And it all flows from a unity of spirit and purpose (verse 32a) which creates an atmosphere in which generosity can flourish.

The passage then reminds us that the foundation for all this is the resurrection (verse 33). It is the pivotal truth on which everything rests. Without the resurrection there would have been no Pentecost, no Spirit-filling, no bold proclamation of the gospel and no sharing lifestyle. As long as they keep on emphasising the resurrection God's favour will be with them (verse 33b).

Such was the power of love in this close-knit community that abject poverty (common in the ancient world) was unknown among them (verse 34a cf. Deut. 15:4). It was not that nobody owned anything, but that they treated possessions so lightly as to be willing to give them up when a need became apparent (verse 32b cf. 34b). You cannot sell things 'from time to time' if you do not own them! Some political and religious groups have tried to see in the early chapters of Acts a pattern for communal living which treated all property and wealth as owned by the group as a whole, not by individuals within it. A careful reading of the passage rejects this conclusion. Nevertheless, community living, where carefully established and led, does provide an excellent opportunity for expressing the teaching of this passage. Most 'average' church life runs the opposite risk – an overly protective attitude to personal possessions, which expresses itself in a narrow view of 'fellowship' and a lack of generosity.

To illustrate this sacrificial sharing, Luke introduces us to Barnabas (verse 36). He is an encourager by name and by nature. 'At the apostles' feet' (verses 35,37) is a phrase used to stress that this is an offering to God, placed at the disposal of the leadership, for the good of all the believers. There is no compulsion here; Barnabas gives in response to need, motivated by compassion.

Questions

1. *Jesus told the 'rich young man' to sell everything he had (Mark 10:21). Does this passage teach that every Christian should do the same? How can we apply the lessons of these verses to our lives today?*

2. *What amount from your church funds is spent on the poor – here and overseas? How can the poor be helped by the church family?*

3. *How can we keep the resurrection of Jesus (verse 33) central to our thinking/living/preaching at times other than Easter?*

Acts 5:1–11

A Major Mistake

Two individuals conspire together to deceive the apostles. God is not fooled! They pay a terrible price for their sinful action.

Ananias and Sapphira, perhaps seeing the high esteem in which Barnabas was held, decided to bring an offering to the apostles. They sold a piece of real estate to make a monetary gift possible (verse 1). What follows is a sad story of human failing and folly. They agree between them that the money is too much to give away; so they will give a proportion of it to the church but claim that it is the total amount received for the property they sold (verse 2). Peter helps them (and us) to see that the sin is *not* giving less than the full amount, but pretending it *is* the full amount. Bringing a smaller offering than they *could* is not wrong; bringing a smaller offering than they claimed they were giving, is! (verse 4).

Ananias is struck dead. Perhaps he had a heart attack at the shock of being found out. If he did, Luke would see this as a secondary cause. For the writer of Acts the primary cause of his death is clear – the judgement of God (verse 5a cf. 12:23). Sapphira then comes in and is given a chance by Peter to tell the truth. She responds with a blatant lie (verse 8). She too is struck dead (verse 10), and buried with her husband; ending her life just three hours after he has ended his (verse 7)! We hardly need to be told by Luke that this incident generated 'fear' among the believers, and in the wider community (verses 5,11).

To modern minds this story comes as something of a shock. Part of this lies in our failure to understand the seriousness of the situation which

Luke records. Peter saw two people, motivated by envy of Barnabas (and others), manipulating God's people for their own ends; they had lied to God (verses 3,4) and attempted to deceive the apostles (verse 2). This betrayal of trust could not go unchallenged. If it had, the new Christian movement could have been derailed in the first stages of its journey. Deceit of this kind would poison relationships, compromise the Christian community and reduce the thrust of its witness. A decisive act is called for. (This passage has parallels in Joshua 7:1–26, where Achan is dealt with in a similarly decisive manner.)

The word 'church' (verse 11) is used for the first time here in Acts, in this passage. A 'mixed-bag' group of believers from many backgrounds and age groups is being welded together as the 'church'. If the new-born church is not to be the still-born church, tough action is necessary against sin of this kind.

Questions

1. *In what ways are we tempted to try to fool God or our church leaders?*

2. *Peter exercised the first church discipline for unacceptable behaviour. Do you think church discipline ought to be exercised more? In what circumstances?*

3. *Do you think we should treat sin more seriously than we do? Why? What would the result be?*

Acts 5:12–16

God's Healing Power

The early Christians operated with a supernatural authority. Healing the sick and releasing people from Satan's grip, were regular features of their work.

Luke reminds us in this passage that despite the threats from the Sanhedrin (4:18,21) and the pressures of internal pastoral problems (e.g. verses 1–11), the church continued to be extremely active. Incredible miracles and supernatural signs of God's activity were the order of the day. It's interesting that Luke thinks of the apostles as the primary agents of the miraculous, rather than individual believers from the rank-and-file of the church (verse 12 cf. 2:43, 4:33) and the major healing incidents recorded all involve the leadership. Every believer had a common purpose and commitment (4:32), each one was filled with the Spirit (2:4, 4:31), all met for worship and prayer (verse 12b cf. 2:46) but apparently only a small group of leaders regularly ministered in this specific 'signs and wonders' way.

Solomon's Colonnade was becoming a regular gathering place for Christians (verse 12b cf. 3:11). They were held in great esteem by the general public, and the church continued to experience significant numerical growth (verse 14). Nevertheless, mixed in with the great esteem was a large portion of fear (verse 13a). You would be wise to avoid that eastern Colonnade if you did not want to be associated with those Christians. The Council had made their view extremely clear and were very influential. Associating with Christians might cost you promotion at work, status in the community ... or worse! Perhaps people started to come to the temple through the western gate, just to be on the safe side. And the incident with Ananias and Sapphira hadn't helped – 'Have you heard about the way they treat you if you step out of line?' – no wonder people were afraid!

But good news spreads, and such is the desperate state of many of the sick and demonised, that they come to the Christians despite the risks. Luke is struck by the fact that the apostles are simply carrying on where Jesus left off. Verse 16 sounds amazingly like Luke 4:37,40. By the power of the Holy Spirit they are continuing the ministry of their Master. All this excitement does seem to have generated some hero-worship of Peter (verse 15) and a somewhat 'magical' view of his healing prowess. It's easy for us to ridicule their primitive and superstitious actions but we should take care! God seems to honour their faith in Him, however naively or crudely it may be expressed. He had healed in similar circumstances in the past (Jesus in Mark 5:28,29) and would do so again in the future (Paul in Acts 19:11,12)!

Questions

1. *Should we expect healing miracles today? Through our leaders (verse 12a)? Any Christian? Where does modern medicine fit in?*

2. *Is your church held in high regard (verse 13b) by the community? How can its standing be improved?*

3. *Some people avoided the early church out of fear (verse 13a). People tend to avoid the church today through 'boredom' or 'irrelevance'. What do you think of this change?*

Acts 5:17–26

Arrest and Escape

Things are hotting up. The apostles are arrested, put in prison, miraculously set free, preach in the temple, and are brought before the Council. All in twenty-four hours!

Motivated by envy at the apostles' standing with the people (verse 17b), the Sadducees have the Christian leadership rounded up and thrown in jail with the common thieves and criminals (verse 18). A night in a prison with characters like these was not an attractive prospect. No doubt the high priest and his cronies were hoping that some mental and physical abuse would soften the apostles up a bit for the next day's hearing! But God had other ideas – a jail-break was arranged, courtesy of an angel (verse 19). The angel instructed them to go back to the temple precinct area and tell the people the good news (verse 20) not missing anything out. (Note the phrase 'full message' (verse 20 N.I.V.).) They are not to tone things down or leave out the controversial bits – despite the pressure and harassment.

The directive of the angel is outrageously audacious, but they do it (verse 21)! So much of this account in the early chapters of Acts contrasts with church life today. They were bold, direct, rude and produced a commotion wherever they went. We are often timid, evasive, overly polite and produce a stifled yawn wherever we go! This description may be a caricature, but an honest assessment of our church life and theirs could not miss the obvious contrast between us.

While the apostles are back in the temple court preaching (verse 21) the security guards are at the prison (verse 22) to bring them to the hearing. This section is not without its humorous side. It has many of the ingredients of a T.V. situation comedy. The security guards are confused (no obvious sign of a break out (verse 23a)), the chief priests 'puzzled' (verse 24b) and everyone on the Sanhedrin (that august and important group!) is embarrassed and wondering how you can have a hearing when there is no one to hear. There is a lot of egg on a lot of faces! Finally the riddle of the missing apostles is solved; an ordinary worshipper has seen them on his way to prayer – they are preaching again (verse 25). At this news, the chief of security and his men go to bring the apostles to the Council. They are gentle and respectful because of the apostles' popularity (verse 26 cf. verse 13).

Much of this echoes the ministry of Jesus, who was often in trouble with the authorities but was followed enthusiastically by the ordinary people (cf. Mark 12:37).

Questions

1. Why do you think the early Church was so different from the Church today? Should we try to change? If so, how?

2. Do you think the 'angel' was a spirit being or a sympathetic jailor (verse 19)? What does Luke think?

3. What kinds of pressures makes us afraid to share the 'full message' (verse 20) with others, in preaching and personal witness?

Acts 5:27-33

Another Trial

The Council is in even more hostile mood the second time round. The apostles repeat their commitment to Jesus and risk the death sentence.

After the fiasco of the night before (verse 18f) the Sanhedrin is in no mood for tolerance. They are desperate to hush this whole thing up before the Romans get wind of it and they are faced with a rebellious group of people who have totally ignored the last court order (4:18 cf. 5:12, 21). In addition, they may have begun to feel the weight of the accusations about their responsibility for the death of Jesus (verse 28 cf. 4:10). Their reputation as a Council would be damaged if they had 'rigged' the death of an innocent man, and if that man was even suspected of being the Messiah ... the implications for their positions and status were too awful to contemplate.

Peter (with the occasional 'hear, hear' from the others) merely restates his position (verse 29 cf. 4:19). They are only doing what God has told them. Once on his feet, Peter treats the Council to another potted sermon, repeating the basic facts of their message. Some of the Sanhedrin have heard this talk before! 'Jesus is more than an ordinary man (verse 31 cf. 2:36, 4:12), you are guilty of killing him (verse 30 cf. 2:36, 4:10), and we have seen Him alive' (verse 32 cf. 2:32, 4:33).

The Council are livid, beside themselves with rage – just as they had been with Jesus (Matt. 26:65). How dare Peter speak to them in this way! His statement implies that they are opposing God, have missed out on recognising the Messiah (even though they were looking for Him), killed the Messiah, are obstructing His work and will not get all God's blessing (the Holy Spirit) until they stop being disobedient and start obeying God (verse 32). And all this delivered by a Galilean nobody, who was more at home with fish than theologians! No wonder they were angry enough to want the apostles killed (verse 33).

This passage helpfully contrasts two groups of leaders. The apostles had genuine integrity; they did not encourage their followers to do one thing and do another themselves. These were not generals who hid behind their troops. They faced threats, harassment, imprisonment, flogging (verse 40), even death (12:2) – no wonder their leadership was respected and followed. By contrast the Sanhedrin had collaborated and compromised with the Romans at every level. Ordinary Jews suffered while they retained their privileges. They had legal 'clout' but no moral authority to rule; they were leaders who had lost the right to lead.

Questions

1. *How can we best support our leaders so that they can be all God wants them to be?*

2. *Peter keeps repeating the basic facts (verses 29–32). What do you think the basic facts of an evangelistic presentation ought to be today?*

3. *Would you have obeyed the Sanhedrin and kept quiet (verse 28)? Can you think of times when you ought to obey God rather than man (verse 29)?*

Acts 5:34–42

Gamaliel to the Rescue

A dramatic intervention in the apostles' trial lessens their punishment; but not even the continued threats can stifle their evangelistic zeal.

The Council may have wanted to put the apostles to death (verse 33) but they did not have the power to do so. Only the occupying power of Rome could sanction the death penalty. They would have to concoct some kind of charge (as they did with Jesus) to convince the Romans that a death sentence was appropriate. They were
deflected from this course of action by one of the most respected religious leaders of the day, a Pharisee named Gamaliel (verse 34). The Pharisees were less influential on the Council than the Sadducees but were still a significant part of the power structure. Gamaliel was widely honoured as an outstanding expert on the law, and a man of high moral character and religious fervour. Presumably he had witnessed the excessive ravings of the Sadducees with some distaste and decided to speak his mind before anything rash was done.

Gamaliel had the defendants removed (verse 36b) so he could speak his mind more easily. He argued that these revolutionary movements come and go. Had not Theudas been seen as a great threat (verse 36)? Now he was dead and the whole thing had blown over; exactly the same had happened to Judas the Galilean (verse 37). 'Don't over-react', he warns them, 'It will all fizzle out'. And he goes on to argue that if it does not, it will be God's will that it succeeds, so you had better not try to oppose God (verse 39)!

It is important not to read too much into the speech. Gamaliel is not on the verge of converting to Christianity. The Pharisees were closer to the apostles theologically than the Sadducees (for example, the Pharisees had a belief in the resurrection) and were less politically compromised. They were religious experts and teachers, often quite poor, and with a reputation for a strict commitment to every detail of the law. They had an overwhelming belief in the will of God (a kind of 'if it happens it must be God's will' mentality) which gave them quite a fatalistic approach to things. Gamaliel's closing words (verse 39) sound very like Peter's (verse 29, cf. verse 19) but the resemblance is superficial. He presents his whole case from the Pharisees' point of view. The Sadducees may not have been persuaded by the logic of Gamaliel's arguments, but they could see the sense in not over-reacting. They had the apostles flogged (39 lashes perhaps – Deut. 25:3), re-issued the court order to be silent, and released them.

The apostles feel privileged to be allowed to suffer for their Lord (verse 41) and completely ignore the court order (verse 42)! The trial and punishment has had the opposite effect from what it was supposed to.

Questions

1. The Pharisees were strict about the letter of the law, yet Jesus criticised them heavily (e.g. Matt. 23:3). Why?

2. Gamaliel rescued the apostles from possible death. Can you think of other occasions (from the Bible or your own experience) when someone who is not a Christian has helped the Christian cause?

3. Do you think we would be better at sharing our faith (verse 42) if we had suffered more (verse 41)?

Acts 6:1–7

Practical Service

The apostles initiate a practical solution to a pastoral problem. Needs are met, new workers are commissioned and the church keeps on growing.

The chapter begins with a reminder that in the early Church things do not stand still – numerical growth continues unabated (verse 1a). This is the fifth specific reference to increase in numbers in these early chapters of Acts; for Luke it's the natural result of a clear presentation of the gospel in the power of the Holy Spirit. He adds a sixth reference (verse 7) at the end of this section and excitedly points out that even the priests are turning to Christ in sizable numbers. For this infant movement to be making inroads into the Establishment is a sign of its power and growing influence. God is on the move!

But the church has an internal pastoral problem to solve. Widows (who had no other means of provision) were cared for from a common purse. However, Jews who spoke mainly Greek (and may well have moved to Jerusalem from another country, leaving themselves cut off from family support) felt that in comparison to the local-born widows, they were getting a bit of a raw deal (verse 1b). We are not told how this happened but the apostles (here given their technical title – 'the twelve') are concerned to put it right (verse 2a) but not at any cost. They must retain their ministry of communicating God's word (verse 2b) if the church is to remain healthy.

They also refuse to impose a solution but suggest, to the whole group, having seven more workers to spread the work-load (verse 3). These men must have had an encounter with God and be wise administrators. Note that the 'spiritual' and 'practical' qualifications are both required. Many a church has appointed a skilled accountant as treasurer but regretted it because of an absence of spirituality! The group agrees with this idea and promptly chooses seven men to ensure that all the different groups in the early church are treated fairly. The seven are then commissioned by the apostles (cf. Num 27:23) by the laying on of hands – a visual aid of the process of giving authority to this group to serve. The group are never described as Deacons by Luke, but do seem to exercise a parallel ministry to that described by Paul in 1 Tim. 3:8–13.

The early Christians were learning what the children of Israel had to learn about leadership – delegate or die (cf. Ex. 18)! More people had to be involved in different aspects of ministry and leadership if the church was to continue growing.

Questions

1. *How can you free your teacher/preacher so that they can give more time to prayer and the ministry of the word (verse 4)?*

2. *What qualifications do you think someone should have before becoming a Deacon?*

3. *Should our churches be growing numerically (verses 1,7)? How can we play our part in this?*

Acts 6:8–15

Stephen's Ministry Takes Off

Newly commissioned as a church worker, Stephen adds miracles and preaching to his duties of a practical nature. God's enemies soon appear, trying to discredit him.

We are not entirely sure why Stephen has such an impact in his ministry of communicating truth and power, when he is supposed to be waiting on tables! Certainly only the apostles have been credited with such amazing power up to this point; they seem to have passed this authority on to Stephen when he was commissioned for ministry (verse 6). It is a clear reminder to us that God is sovereign and perfectly capable of using people in any way He wants. We may not think a waiter should have a powerful miracle-ministry, but God might. We must not restrict Him.

Opposition soon turns up, apparently from those who shared Stephen's Greek language and cultural background. These Jews call themselves free (verse 9 'freed men') but are bound by prejudice and fear of this new teaching. They try to argue with this Christian worker but he has been well taught by the apostles and speaks with the power of the Spirit. They cannot defeat his argument (verse 10), but where logic and truth fail them, deceit and treachery come to their rescue – they recruit some false witnesses, lobby the religious leadership and kidnap Stephen to bring him to the Council. (Not a body of men noted for their warmth towards the Christians – see 5:18, 5:33). Things continue to go downhill for Stephen as the false witnesses repeat and enlarge on their allegations in front of the

Sanhedrin (verse 13). Their charges are not so much complete fabrications as grotesque distortions of what he had said. (They had made precisely the same charge about Jesus (Matt. 26:61) twisting His words.) Despite all this pressure he still remains calm and assured – God's Spirit giving him the appearance of an angel (verse 15). There is more than a touch of irony here: Moses is under threat, Stephen's accusers say, and yet the description of Stephen parallels that of Moses having just had his meeting with God (Ex. 34:29).

Notice how the freed men are totally unconcerned about whether the message of Stephen is true or not. It threatens their position and perhaps even their safety (what if people assume they are linked with Stephen because of their shared culture and language?); Stephen must be stopped. Truth must not be allowed to get in the way of comfort and security!

Questions

1. *Are you stuck in one ministry, because you believe God cannot use you for anything else? How can we recognise when ministries are changing or developing – in ourselves and others?*

2. *How do you feel when you are being lied about (see verse 13)? How should you feel ... and react?*

3. *How do we behave when our comfort and security are threatened? How can we be open to new ideas, correction or anything else which makes us feel vulnerable?*

Acts 7:1–8

Stephen Begins his Defence

The longest speech in the book of Acts begins. Stephen describes some highlights from Jewish history – starting with Abraham – all leading to Jesus.

After hearing from the accusers (6:13,14), the high priest turns his attention to the defence. Stephen is invited to confess his guilt or deny it (verse 1); he chooses to launch into a major speech, drawing on significant portions of the Old Testament to establish his case. It's important to understand that this is not an academic lecture on Jewish history. Some important incidents are missed out and some of the information seems a bit muddled when we look back to the Old Testament itself. This is a man arguing for his life in the cauldron of treachery which the Council meeting had become. We are a million miles from the detached objectivity of the lecture room! The thrust of the argument is what is vital, not the neat arrangement of the material.

After a respectful, almost warm, greeting (verse 2 'brothers and fathers'), Stephen begins his defence with Abraham, one of the earliest and most significant people in all of Jewish history. Stephen describes how *faith* played a significant part in Abraham's life. Without knowing where he was going (verse 3 cf. Gen. 12:1) he was to set off! Given all the dangers of travel in the ancient world, this journey would have been reckless, even foolish, had it not been a step of faith in response to a word from God. (There are important lessons here. To act 'in faith' when God has *not* spoken is reckless and irresponsible. To not act when He *has* spoken is disobedient and faithless. Listen and obey).

Abraham also had to exercise faith when he arrived in the land he was promised. He would not see the fulfilment in his own life-time, but his descendants (after a period in Egypt, see Gen. 15:13,14) would inherit the land (verses 4–7). The covenant of circumcision was then given as a sign of the special relationship between God and Abraham and his descendants (verse 8). Rom. 4:9f is Paul's development of Stephen's argument. Abraham exercised faith, which led to circumcision; he did not believe because of circumcision, circumcision was given because he believed!

All this seems immensely complicated to us. We need to remember that their history was very, very important to the Jews. Their ancestors were not just figures of interest, but role-models to follow. 'If Abraham did it so should we'. Stephen is trying to demonstrate that if they want to be good Jews they should remember not only the *result* of Abraham's relationship with God (they were absorbed by the rite of circumcision and the possession of the land) but also the *cause* of it. (Faith and obedience, cf. 3:17, 4:19).

Questions

1. How can we discern the difference between faith and foolishness? How can we help each other?

2. What can we learn from our own history – the story of the church? Why is it important?

3. How can we make sure we do not get absorbed in the work of the Lord but forget the Lord of the work?

Acts 7:9–19

Stephen's Defence Continues

Stephen, warming to his theme, discusses the lives of Joseph and Moses.
The foundation stones for the arrival of Jesus continue to be laid.

Moving on from Abraham, Stephen takes the Council into
the life of Joseph. His brothers (verse 9 'patriarchs' = sons
of Jacob) hated him because they were jealous of his
favour with his father (Gen. 34:3) and his vivid dreams
which showed them bowing down to him (Gen. 34:10,11).
God was not deflected from His purpose for Joseph, He

simply used a heathen ruler in a foreign country to provide for him (verse
10). Such was God's care for His people that he told Joseph to prepare for
famine seven years before it happened (Gen. 41:25–32) and made sure his
father heard about this provision at the right time (verses 11,12 cf. Gen.
42:2). Despite this famine, and the later deceit and oppression of the
Pharaoh (verse 19) God continued to provide for His people.

The thrust of Stephen's argument was that God was bigger than the
Jews' obsession with their land. Stephen does not deny that they have been
promised the land, simply that God is not limited by it or constrained
within it. He had provided for His people in Joseph's day in *another* land
('Egypt' is mentioned *eight* times in the passage, as if to underline this!). By
focussing so fully on the promise of the land the contemporaries of
Stephen are in danger of reducing God to a localised deity, with little
interest in anything beyond some narrow geographical boundaries!

So much of later Christian teaching flows from this argument. Stephen
could not have realised the significance of his speech for, for example, the

concept of the God of the whole world (17:24–28) and the place of non-Jews in the purpose of God (11:1f). Both these themes are picked up and developed later in Acts. Stephen is describing Jewish history in a way which challenges their traditional understanding. He wants to demonstrate that, in his understanding of Jewish history, the arrival of Jesus the Messiah should not have been a total surprise. God has been hinting at it since Abraham, and getting increasingly obvious in those hints as Jewish history moves on through Joseph to Moses.

The Council must have been irritated at this lesson from Jewish history, delivered by someone with a Greek name, who had been appointed to 'wait on tables' (6:2)! Worse was to come.

Questions

1. 'My country, right or wrong.' What does this passage imply about an attitude like this?

2. Stephen's speech is heavily based on the Old Testament. Why do you think it is so neglected by Christians? How can we change this?

3. Joseph repaid jealousy (verse 9) with food (verses 13,14). Would you have done? Why do we find 'forgiving and forgetting' so hard?

Acts 7:20–32

Stephen's Defence – Part Three

Stephen's speech focuses on Moses, perhaps the most respected figure in Jewish history. The evidence for Jesus the Messiah continues to grow.

Stephen begins by reminding the Council of the miraculous preservation of Moses in the early months of his life (verses 20, 21 cf. Ex. 2:1–10). He honours his great stature ('no ordinary child') and his gifting (verse 22 – 'powerful in speech and action'). Stephen may well have had the comments of his accusers in mind (6:11,14) when he speaks of Moses in such glowing terms.

What follows in the next verses picks up the theme begun in the last section. God is bigger than their concern about the Land – their beloved Palestine. Moses was born outside it (verse 20), educated outside it (verse 22), had a home outside it (9:29), was commissioned outside it (verse 30) and exercised his ministry outside it (verse 34). Egypt, Midian, Mount Sinai and Egypt again, were all places where God was obviously present and chose to act decisively and powerfully. Of course, all these facts would be known to the Council, but the *implications* of these facts had either been missed or ignored. Stephen's case here hangs on his interpretation of history. One particular aspect of God's plan (His promise of the land) has been emphasised to the detriment of many other parts of His purpose (e.g. the coming of the Messiah). Stephen's contemporaries have read the Old Testament through the 'tinted lenses' of the 'land pre-occupation' – he invites them to take off their glasses and give the material a fresh look!

One of the small phrases in this passage which we should not miss occurs when Stephen speaks of the 'wisdom of the Egyptians' (verse 22) so positively. The Jews were an insular race who would have found the thought of wisdom in other cultures difficult to take; especially when it was a culture they loved to hate. Emphasising that their beloved Moses was dependent on a foreign culture for his education (and a foreign woman for his upbringing) must have stuck in their throats. Religious purity was one thing, but first century Judaism often descended into a narrow nationalism. Stephen is obviously committed to the separation which protects from compromise, but not to a separation which produced bigotry and arrogance.

Notice also the short phrase in verse 30 – 'after forty years'. Moses waited a long time before God's purpose was revealed. We do well to remind ourselves that God's timetable may be different from ours (2 Peter 3:8,9)!

Questions

1. *Why do countries seem to believe in the superiority of their own citizens? Is this justifiable pride or national arrogance?*

2. *Do we have a particular issue that colours all we think? (Ask your friends!) How can we read the Bible 'without prejudice'?*

3. *What does the patience of Moses (verse 30) have to teach us about answers to prayer?*

Acts 7:33–50

Stephen Concluding his Speech

Stephen continues with Moses and then moves on through the tabernacle to the temple. He completes his survey of the Old Testament.

The passage begins with the theme of rejection (verse 35). This has been hinted at before in the speech (Joseph – verse 9, Moses – verse 25) and is going to be one of the major points in Stephen's summing up. And this rejection of Moses was not confined to the start of his ministry. Even after incredible miracles, the plagues and the crossing of the Red Sea, they still reject him as leader (verse 36). In the process they reject his deliverance from Egypt (verse 39b) and they reject his God (verses 40–42). This whole sorry stage in Israelite history (which sowed the seeds for future idolatry and rebellion – verses 42,43 cf. Amos 5:25–27) occurred because God's chosen rescuer, Moses, was rejected.

'Make no mistake about it', Stephen says, 'Moses was great, really great (verses 20,22,36) but he pointed forward to someone else' (verse 37). This person would be one of them, a Jew, with a rescue-ministry, just like Moses. (You can almost feel the Sanhedrin getting increasingly concerned and irritated as the implications of some of these statements begin to dawn on them!)

Moses had just received the Law (verse 38) – 'Living words' Stephen calls them – when the rejection of Moses and the idolatry began. Stephen's two words to describe the Law indicate his belief in their divine origin and in their relevance to human life. His accusers were wide off the mark (6:13); his view of the Law was not destructive or negative.

In the years which followed the life of Moses, God's presence was identified with a large tent (the tabernacle). This went with the people of Israel in the wilderness (verse 44), over the Jordan and into the promised land (verse 45a). It lasted through the entire period of the Judges, through Saul's kingship and David's (verse 45b) until he proposed a temple to replace it (verse 46). The project was completed by David's son, Solomon (verse 47). However, God was bigger than the splendid temple built for Him (verses 48,49 cf. Isaiah 66:1); it could not contain Him. He had created everything (verse 50 cf. Isaiah 66:2) – not even heaven and earth were big enough!

The Jews placed great emphasis on the Law and the Temple. Stephen points out the limitations of both. The Law (even with Moses present!) did not stop a full-scale rebellion against God. The Temple (magnificent though it was) could not begin to contain the Almighty. None of the traditional emphases were enough to express all of God.

Questions

1. *Can a Christian worship an idol (see verse 41)? What do 'idols' look like in the 1990s?*

2. *Is our God too small? In what ways do we try to limit or contain Him?*

3. *In what ways do we reject God's messengers today? what are the results (see verses 39,40)?*

Acts 7:51–8:1a

Stephen – The First Martyr

Stephen brings his defence to a passionate conclusion. The Council's verdict is 'death'. God's verdict is 'glory'!

And so Stephen concludes his speech. He has painstakingly built up his evidence to arrive at the conclusion that the excessive preoccupation of his contemporaries with the Land, the Law and the Temple (worthy though they are) has blinded them to the significance of Jesus the Messiah (verses 2–50). Despite claiming to be students of the Old Testament, they have missed, ignored or misunderstood this vital strand in its teaching.

In these verses Stephen moves from defence to attack. Using language reminiscent of the ancient prophets (cf. Ex. 33:5, Isaiah 63:10), he accuses them of being just like the rebellious Israelites of old. Like their ancestors they resist God (verse 51b) and reject His messengers (verse 52a) and have now gone so far as to reject the Messiah – by killing Him (verse 52b)! (This last accusation must have stung. The Council has heard it *twice* before from Peter (4:10, 5:30). What is more, even by their own standards ('the Law' – verse 53) they have disobeyed God.

They are wild with anger (Christians seemed to have this effect on the Sanhedrin, cf. 5:33) contorting their faces and mouths in rage (verse 54). Stephen, by contrast, is serene and peaceful; a vision of his Messiah with God the Father (verse 55) fills his mind. (The words of Jesus in Mark 14:62 may well have prompted this experience.) The Council can stand it no longer. They cover their ears, scream abuse at Stephen and drag him off to be bludgeoned to death by rocks and stones at the edge of the city (verses 57,58).

Stephen dies as he has lived, filled with the Holy Spirit (verse 55), with a prayer on his lips for his killers (verse 60) and a commitment of himself back to God (verse 59). In many ways he reminds us of Jesus: his lack of resistance, his serene spirit and his dying words (cf. Luke 23:34,46). He is the first Christian martyr, he will not be the last. His courage and bearing have strengthened many down the centuries in their final hours.

Twice in this section, Luke mentions someone who will come to dominate the last part of Acts and tower over the development of the early church. He is a young man named Saul (verse 58b, 8:1a). He guards the cloaks of the executioners and approves of the death of this Christian 'heretic'. But God will have the final word in his life!

Questions

1. How can we learn to forgive our enemies when we feel more like revenge?

2. Do you think Stephen's example played a part in Saul's conversion? List the people who played a part in yours and thank God for them.

3. Would you be prepared to die for your faith? Lose your job? Your friends? What priority does our faith have in our lives? What can we do to help people in countries where these things often happen?

Acts 8:1b–8

Persecution and Power

. **Stephen's death releases a tidal wave of persecution and harassment for the early Christians. Philip escapes the trouble but keeps on proclaiming the gospel.**

The stoning of Stephen seems to have unleashed all the pent-up frustration and anger which was felt by many Orthodox Jews. Jerusalem had ceased to be a safe place for followers of Jesus, so they found themselves fleeing into the countryside and towns around the city (Judea) or pushing further north to settle in Samaria (verse 16). The apostles (probably 'the twelve') remained in the city to continue to provide a headquarters for the developing Christian movement. It is not clear how they avoided arrest. Perhaps they were in semi-hiding, protected by the goodwill of ordinary people, (cf. 5:13).

Stephen is not forgotten. 'Godly men' (verse 2) gave him a decent burial and there was obviously much sadness. Luke seems to imply that these men were not part of the early church. They could have been Pharisees (like Gamaliel) who felt that the Council's reaction had been rash and ill-advised. It is possible that remorse may have set in among more 'open', sensitive members of the Sanhedrin. Certainly no such remorse appeared to be worrying Saul, who threw himself into persecuting the church with systematic, hateful enthusiasm (verse 3). This was a door-to-door campaign of a different sort! No-one was safe from his violence; homes and privacy were violated, even the women received no mercy.

While all this was going on, one of Stephen's colleagues on the diaconate had found his way to Samaria (verse 5). Like other Christian refugees (verse 4) Philip gave himself whole-heartedly to the evangelistic task. Just like Stephen (6:8) he found he had a far wider and more powerful ministry than food distribution. The apostles' commissioning (6:6) had released power and new ministries in him (cf. 2 Tim. 1:6). The expressions of healing power made people pay 'close attention' (verse 6) to his message. Various individuals were released from crippling physical conditions and the grip of Satan was broken in many lives (verse 7). No wonder they were delighted to have him (verse 8)!

The amazing irony is that the persecution is having the opposite effect from the one intended. Far from being contained, the gospel message is spreading; just as Jesus said it would (1:8 cf. 8:1). And to the Samaritans of all people, sworn enemies of the Jews; they hated each other (cf. John 4:9)! The Good News is already crossing cultural, religious and racial boundaries, bringing healing and forgiveness.

Questions

1. Which countries/groups are trying to 'destroy the church' (verse 3)? How would you feel if they were persecuting Christians 'house to house' (verse 3) in your town?

2. Do you think there is great joy (verse 8) in your community because of the Christians who live there? Why/why not?

3. Does your church make judgements on the basis of race? (Do you?!) What does the New Testament in general (e.g. Col. 3:11) and Acts in particular teach about this?

Acts 8:9-14

Simon the 'Magician'

Philip continues his ministry and comes into contact with a local 'sorcerer'. The apostles arrive to lend a hand and encourage Philip.

Luke now introduces us to a new character: Simon. Philip may have seen Simon as a rival for the attention of the Samaritans. Both of them do astounding things which amaze the people ... but there the similarity ends. Simon's displays of wonder are called 'magic' (verse 11), Philip's are called 'miracles' (verse 13), Simon talks about himself (verse 9b), Philip talks about God (verse 12); after Simon's 'magic' people follow *him* (verse 11a), after Philip's 'miracles' people follow Jesus (verse 12b)!

That Simon could do amazing tricks was not in question. Even assuming that the people of Samaria were a little gullible, we are still dealing with an impressive personality displaying remarkable powers. The Samaritans certainly thought he was some kind of god (verse 10b) or at least, the special representative of a god. He cannot have been thrilled when the people switch allegiance to Philip and his message about the kingdom of God. Simon is very impressed by Philip's power and hovers at his side constantly (verse 13b), presumably to work out how the 'magic' works. Simon has seen the people's response to Philip (verse 12b) and assumes that this is the first step to getting Philip's power; he himself is baptised (verse 13a).

It is very difficult indeed to know if Simon's 'conversion' is genuine. Surely Philip would have spotted a 'con' or act of pretence? On the other hand, his motives don't seem to be pure (like those in Jesus' day (John

2:23–25) who 'believed' on the basis of the miracles they had seen. Jesus did not trust them!) nor does the description which Peter gives him (verses 20–23) easily fit someone who is a genuine believer. Perhaps he is so obsessed with his search for power that he is partially blinded to his own motives; he believes in Jesus to obtain another source of power. God will not be used in this way.

When the apostles in Jerusalem (verse 1b) hear about how the gospel is making inroads into the Samaritan community, they send Peter and John to check it out (verse 14). It would have been thrilling for them to see the words of Jesus coming true (1:8) and the gospel being released among their (previously hated) northern neighbours. Peter and John are keen to witness this remarkable development with their own eyes. The Samaritan believers would need to be assured of their acceptance, and given an apostolic stamp of approval!

Questions

1. *Do we follow Jesus because it makes us happy? Secure? – or because it's true?*

2. *Is there a group of people near your church who are resented/ mistrusted by the community as a whole (e.g. an ethnic minority, travellers, etc.)? How can God's love be shared with them?*

3. *Should we see more evidence of the miraculous in our evangelism (verses 6,13)? What difference would it make? What dangers would there be to avoid?*

Acts 8:15–25

Peter Clashes with Simon

After meeting the new converts, Peter and John introduce them to the Holy Spirit's power. Simon's manipulation is confronted and exposed.

The 'normal' pattern of believing in Jesus and receiving the Spirit seems to have been altered on this occasion (verses 15–17). It's doubtful that Philip's ministry is defective and they have to wheel in the big guns to put it right. More likely, the Spirit is withheld until a closer bonding between Jerusalem believers and Samaritan believers can be expressed in the presence of Peter and John. At this stage in the expansion of Christianity it would be devastating for the Samaritans to encounter the Spirit without 'encountering' their fellow Jewish believers. Baptism is into one body (1 Cor. 12:13) not two – Jewish Christians and Samaritan Christians. 'Normally', believing and receiving would happen together; this unique missionary situation needed an alternative pattern.

When Simon saw the power of Peter and John (he seems to have been a spectator not a participant) he attempts to buy their apostolic status (verse 18) so that he too can release the power of the Spirit into people's lives (verse 19). There seems to have been some visible sign as the apostles prayed (tongues? vibrant joy? great emotion?) and no doubt Simon also believed it to be the key which unlocked the kind of power he had seen Philip exercise (verse 13).

Peter rounds on Simon immediately with a blunt condemnation of both his action (verse 20) and his attitude (verse 21). (Actually he seems to get away with it quite lightly compared with Ananias and Sapphira – 5:1–11!)

The apostles cannot be 'bought' and neither can God's power. Repentance is Simon's only hope (verse 22). Far from being someone great (verse 9b) he was a slave, in bondage to his own motives and desires; full of smouldering resentments (verse 23) Simon is stunned by this verbal assault, but not motivated to repentance. His request to Peter is only an attempt to avoid further punishment; he shows no sign of a genuine change of heart (verse 24).

This story acts as a potent reminder of the dangers of counterfeit faith. So much about Simon seems to indicate a change of heart (verse 13a). How many of us have known those who make some kind of 'decision' for Christ, they may even have made it to baptism or confirmation, but who soon reveal their faith as defective? Their 'decision' was to please a parent, get a child baptised or continue a relationship – Jesus was never the end, only the means!

Peter and John returned south to Jerusalem taking the opportunity to evangelise as they went (verse 25). What exciting news they had to share with their fellow apostles – the gospel was spreading and the church was growing.

Questions

1. *Jealousy played a big part in Simon's downfall. Why is it so dangerous? How do we spot it in ourselves? What can we do to conquer it?*

2. *Is it possible to be filled with the Spirit and hate your neighbour or a fellow church member? Why/why not?*

3. *In what ways do people 'use' the church or God for their own purposes? How can we discern when this is happening?*

Acts 8:26–40

Philip and the Ethiopian

Philip is supernaturally commissioned to meet an Ethiopian, to witness to him. Conversion and baptism follow his presentation of the Good News.

Fresh from the excitement of the crowds in Samaria, Philip is now given a divine assignment to an individual. It is about fifty miles from Jerusalem to Gaza, and the road runs through desert as it heads south, reaching the city of Gaza itself (verse 26). As he travels, Philip meets up with an African from the South Sahara (Sudan?) who is chancellor of the exchequer for Candace, (a title not a name) ruler of Ethiopia (verse 27a). He is a 'eunuch' (though probably this is an official title, not a physical description, denoting the removal of his sexual organs) and must have been a convert to Judaism, because he has been up to Jerusalem to worship (verse 27b) and he has obtained a copy of Isaiah (verse 28) – both would be extremely difficult for a Gentile. (Besides, Luke views Cornelius as the first gentile convert, 11:1.)

Prompted by the Holy Spirit (verse 29) Philip approaches this high-ranking official and starts chatting about the book the Ethiopian seems to be about two thirds of the way through. 'Do you understand Isaiah 53:7,8?', Philip asks (verse 30). 'No, but climb in and tell me about it', he replies (verse 31). This important man is gracious and humble, obviously ready to lear.., so Philip uses Isaiah to point the way to Jesus. Stephen has already used the Old Testament to the same effect with a crowd (the Council); now Philip uses the same technique with an individual (verse

35). Jesus is the key to understanding the Old Testament Scriptures; they, in turn, point forward to His coming.

The message of Philip is obviously heard and understood, and baptism is requested when he sees an oasis by the side of the road (verse 36). After the baptism Philip disappears (adding a supernatural ending (verse 39) to a story with a supernatural start – verse 26) and continues his preaching ministry to the north in Azotus. From there he travels north, evangelising coastal towns on the sixty mile journey to Caesarea (verse 40). The Ethiopian cannot see Philip but he can 'see' Jesus! He returns to Africa 'rejoicing' (verse 39) in his newly found faith.

The gospel makes another advance: first the Jews, then the Samaritans, now a black African in a position of great influence. Jesus certainly died (see verses 32,33) but he is not dead – His power and message continue to change lives.

Questions

1. *Baptism is obviously important in Acts (verse 36 cf. 2:38,41). Have you been baptised? Why is it important?*

2. *Notice the three divine 'nudges' Philip got in this story (verses 26,29,39). Why is it important to be sensitive to the Holy Spirit in evangelism? How can we learn to listen to Him as we witness?*

3. *Isaiah was talking about Jesus (verse 34) and so was Philip (verse 35). Who are we talking about? Does Jesus feature strongly in our conversations and lives?*

A gospel for everyone

Jesus leaves His disciples with a promise and a command (1:8) about the spread of the Good News. It is a remarkable statement to make to Jews, who in the main, saw God's blessing reserved for them. As the story of the church unfolds in Acts, we see the gospel reaching out to more and more people. These people are not only distant from Jerusalem geographically, but also in culture, religion, race and colour.

Luke shows us the message of Jesus breaking down barriers of every kind. The hated Samaritans respond to the Good News (8:4f cf. John 4:9), a black African Eunuch is converted (8:26f), as is an 'unclean' Gentile (10:44-48) ... and women discover Christ (9:36) and are used by Him in ministry (21:9)! Almost all the prejudices of a first-century Jew are confronted. No-one is barred, everyone is welcome, the gospel knows no 'exclusion zones'.

Acts 9:1–9

Saul Turned Around

A persistent persecutor of God's people is stopped in his tracks. Jesus confronts Saul on the road to Damascus – a dramatic conversion results.

Saul may well have been more moved by the death of Stephen than he cares to admit (see 7:58, 8:1). But if he was he certainly is not admitting it to anyone – especially not himself! He redoubles his already fanatical harassment of the Christians (verse 1) by asking permission to go into Eastern Syria, to one of the major towns, in order to continue his mission (verse 2). The Jewish Council had no authority politically in Syria, but would have had significant influence over the *Jews* living in Damascus (there may have been over 20,000 at this stage of the first century). Saul is determined to bring to 'justice' all these followers of 'the Way' (cf. John 14:6) – they need not think that by running over a hundred and fifty miles away, they would escape detection!

As Saul got near to the end of his journey to Damascus, he was put in God's spotlight in no uncertain terms (verse 3). Light more sudden and bright than lightning, 'knocked' him to the ground and a voice enquired about why Saul was persecuting him (verse 4). Saul is no doubt very confused (this seems to be God's voice, but Saul is not persecuting God, but defending His honour; isn't he?!) and not a little afraid. In a state of confusion and fear he stutters out a request to know the identity of the voice (verse 5a). He must have been totally stunned by the reply (verse 5b), devastated emotionally by the implications of the words. All this time he has been opposing the work of God, doing the opposite of what he thought he was doing. For a man of Saul's intensity, all this must have been an incredible shock to the system.

The voice (Jesus) then tells Saul to go into Damascus and wait for further instructions (verse 6). All this time his assistants were stunned into silence; they heard vague sounds, but could not eavesdrop on the conversation between Saul and Jesus, or see anyone but Saul (verse 7). Saul staggers to his feet, only to discover that the light has blinded him (verse 8). This gives him no choice but to obey the voice, spending three days recovering from the shock and trying to work out what it all means (verse 9). Saul, the strong, confident persecutor has met his match.

Questions

1. 'It doesn't matter what you believe as long as you are sincere'. What does this passage have to say about this statement? What would you say if someone said it to you?

2. Should we all have a 'Damascus Road' experience? Does conversion need to be dramatic?

3. When was the last time you took three days to think about something?! Do you think Christians should spend more time 'reflecting' than they tend to? Why?

Acts 9:10-19a

Ananias and Saul

Saul needs help, and God provides it through a faithful disciple – Ananias. Saul is a changed man: through God's power and the obedience of Ananias.

Ananias seems to have lived in Damascus for some time, although how he became a Christian we are not told. He was obviously a committed follower of Jesus whom God spoke to in a vision (9:10) with instructions about Saul (verses 11,12). Saul was a broken man – spiritually turned around, emotionally stunned and physically disabled – but Ananias has only a hint of all this. He can hardly believe that God is sending him into the lion's den ... to help the lion! 'Don't you know, Lord, this is the man who has damaged your church in Jerusalem and has come here to do the same?' (verses 13,14).

The Lord did know this, and still wants Ananias to go! Saul was to be a key agent for God's kingdom. He would preach before Jews and Gentiles, even having opportunities to address their rulers (verse 15). But this high calling would have its cost: Saul would not have a life of ease and comfort (verse 16). So Ananias went. It is important to understand the courage and level of obedience of the Damascan disciple. Would he be ambushed by Saul's assistants? Once in the house of Judas (verse 11) how would he get out? How would his fellow Christians feel about him helping their sworn enemy? Despite all these questions (and the anxiety that went with them!) Ananias still does what Jesus tells him.

Saul is praying (verse 11b) and Ananias immediately affirms him as a brother in Christ (verse 17). He has come on the instruction of Jesus to bring physical healing and spiritual release (verse 17b). Luke does not tell us about what (if any) signs followed Saul's filling with the Spirit (cf. 2:4, 4:31) but it is certain the prayer of Ananias was effective. Saul's physical sight is restored (verse 18a) and his new spiritual sight is expressed in baptism (verse 18b). ('Straight street' (verse 11) was a prestigious road with substantial housing – perhaps there was a pool in the courtyard). Once he starts to eat again (verse 19) he returns to full physical health and strength.

The order of events – Holy Spirit filling followed by baptism – is the reverse of the Samaritan experience (8:12,17). It is hard to escape the conclusion that in these early days of church life, the *order* of events in becoming a Christian is nowhere near as important as the *reality* of each component part.

Questions

1. *Would you have been as obedient as Ananias? What would make you hesitate? How can we strengthen our courage?*

2. *Why is there so much emphasis in Acts on being filled with the Holy Spirit (verse 17)? Is there too much or too little emphasis on this today?*

3. *For Saul, success and suffering would go hand in hand (verses 15,16). Is this a 'rule' of the Christian life? Do you think our lack of success is because of our fear of suffering?*

Acts 9:19b-31

An Enthusiastic Convert

Saul, now physically strong and spiritually empowered, preaches passionately about Jesus. He stirs up opposition and distrust, before being accepted by the Christians.

This is a really remarkable about-face. After a few days consulting with the Christian community in Damascus (verse 19) Saul launches into a vigorous and enthusiastic proclamation of the gospel. In what appears to be little more than a week, he has gone from being a Christ-deny- ing, bigoted Pharisee to announcing to the Jewish community that Jesus really is the Christ. An amazing 'U-turn!' Only the power of God can explain this.

So incredible is this conversion that both the Jews (verse 21) and the Christians (verse 26) had trouble believing it! Now nobody trusts him easily. But Saul is unstoppable; his religious education and training coupled with his dramatic experience make him a formidable debater against the orthodox Jewish opposition (verse 22). He could show 'beyond reasonable doubt' ('proving' – verse 22b) that Jesus was who He said he was. The sound of the Pharisee-turned-traitor becomes too much for the Jews to bear, so they plan to have him killed (verses 23,24). Their plot is foiled by the clever use of a basket and some rope (verse 25); not a very dignified method of transport for a religious leader but Saul is going to have to get used to far worse things in the future!

Luke is only giving us a summary of Saul's life at this point – not every detail. He tells us nothing about going to Arabia (Gal. 1:17) and then back to Damascus. When Luke writes his account he is not concerned to fill in all the biographical details of Saul's life – these are simply the 'recorded highlights'. It is three years before Saul arrives in Jerusalem (Gal. 1:18) and even then he is treated with suspicion. Fortunately Barnabas the encourager is on hand to act as go-between. Barnabas tells them about Saul's experience of Jesus (verse 27) and Saul is accepted by the Jerusalem church. He continues to preach and debate about Jesus, but his life is threatened again (verse 29). The Believers decide that for his own safety he ought to be out of Jerusalem; they send him home to Tarsus (verse 30 cf. verse 11).

This is followed by a period of relative calm in the relationship between the Christians and the Jews (verse 31a). The church uses this time to recover from persecution, God graciously continues to give encouraging signs of His presence and numerical growth results (verse 31).

Questions

1. *Can the people you know who most hate Christianity, be converted? How should this passage affect our prayer life?*

2. *Barnabas brought the two sides together (verse 27). Why is the ministry of reconciliation so important? How can we encourage it?*

3. *Sometimes it's right to stay and fight (e.g. 5:40,41), sometimes to leave the trouble-spot (verse 30). How can we know when to do what?*

Acts 9:32–43

Peter's Power Ministry

Peter visits two key cities in his evangelistic travels. A healing and a 'resurrection' result in many discovering Jesus and following Him.

Luke picks up the story of Peter where he left him (8:25) – preaching the gospel. He goes to a town twenty-five miles northwest of Jerusalem to encourage the Christians (verse 32). He discovers a man who is so badly paralysed that he has been bed-bound for eight years. Peter heals him, in the name of Jesus (verse 34 cf. 3:6) and tells him to put his sleeping mat away; from now on he will only need it at night! Aeneas was a remarkable testimony to God's healing power, and lots of people in Lydda and northward into neighbouring Sharon, came to Christ as a result (verse 35).

Thirty five miles away at the port of Joppa, a very special lady was dying. This woman was always making clothing for the poor and caring for them in a range of different ways (verses 36,39b). With no state provision, widows were often some of the poorest members of the community (cf. James 1:27); no wonder they were so distraught when she died (verse 39). Dorcas would be badly missed. The Believers in Joppa respond to this emergency by sending two of their number inland to ask Peter to come from Lydda (verse 38). Peter may well have remembered how Jesus dealt with the daughter of Jairus (Mark 5:38–42) because he handles the situation in a very similar way ... and the result is the same!

Peter then presents the very alive Dorcas to two significant groups: the Christians to encourage their faith and the widows to assure them of further help in the fight against poverty (verse 41). Both groups – perhaps for different reasons – would have been thrilled. The result of this 'resurrection' was a significant rise in the number of Christians in the region (verse 42 cf. John 12:10,11. The raising of Lazarus had similar results). Peter then stayed on in Joppa, presumably to assist with the discipleship of the new converts and to continue preaching the gospel. He was even happy to stay with Simon, whose contact with dead animals made him 'unclean' as far as the Jewish Rabbis were concerned. In addition, the tanner's job was often associated with dirt and a pungent smell; the general population may have avoided him for this reason.

So Peter stays with Simon (verse 43). A man rejected by the Jews and snubbed by the rest of the community, finds acceptance in the Christian church.

Questions

1. *Do you think that Peter was able to raise Dorcas because he used the same method as Jesus? Similar words? or was it something else?*

2. *Dorcas ministered to the 'poor' (verse 36). Who are the 'poor' in your town? The world? How can you help?*

3. *Simon the tanner was an outcast, yet Peter identified with him (verse 43). Which groups of people are snubbed in your community? How can you identify with them?*

Acts 10:1–8

Cornelius and the Angel

A Roman centurion receives angelic help in his spiritual journey. He asks Peter to come from Joppa – a Gentile asking help from a Jew.

This next section in Acts describes a major advance in the spread of the gospel. Jews with a Hebrew or Greek background (6:1), the 'half-Jews' of Samaria (8:1), an African–Jewish convert (8:27) ... and now a Gentile. It is nothing short of a miracle that a faith which grew out of Judaism could be offered to Gentiles so quickly!

Cornelius lived in the port of Caesarea (verse 1), the Roman capital of Judea which was about sixty five miles northwest of Jerusalem. It needed a Roman cohort (up to about six hundred men) to protect the harbour area, the city's administrative buildings and the vital water supply, brought by aquaduct into the city. Cornelius was neither a Jew nor a Jewish convert, but he was a kind, generous and deeply religious man (verse 2), and so were his family. During mid-afternoon prayer, in broad daylight, he saw an angel (verse 3) who calls him by name. It is all he can do to stutter out a simple question (a very similar response to Saul – 9:5) in his panic (verse 4). God had noted his kindness to the poor and his spiritual devotion. He is told to send for Peter, who is thirty miles away in Joppa, living by the sea-shore (verse 6). They would have had to ask for Simon's house when they arrived in Joppa – or perhaps they just followed their noses! (See comments on 9:43).

Many of Cornelius' servants obviously share his spiritual leanings, as do some of his soldiers (verse 7); after sharing his 'angelic' experience, he sends three of them off on the errand (verse 8). The soldiers' presence is for physical protection but also to add a certain 'official' authority as they travelled; and particularly as they tried to obtain accommodation on the way and directions to Simon's house, once in Joppa.

It is interesting to note that both of the last two characters in Luke's account of the growth of the church (Dorcas and Cornelius) have two things in common. Firstly, they are both in groups of people you would never expect to be commended in a Jewish culture – women and Gentiles. It is almost as if the gospel delights in working with the under-dog! (See comment on 4:13). Secondly, they are both commended for their work among the poor (9:36, verse 4), an activity which always has the blessing of Jesus because it was part of His ministry (Luke 4:18).

Questions

1. How can we help the poor – the starving, the refugee, etc. – in the world? What can your church do?

2. Prayer plays an important part in the life of Cornelius (verses 2,3). What state is your prayer life in? How can it be developed?

3. Cornelius is in the army (verse 1). Why do some people believe that military service is not right for Christians? How should we relate to those who disagree with us about this?

Acts 10:9–23a

Peter's Revolutionary Vision

Peter is spoken to by God in a powerful way, changing the scope of his missionary activity. God uses a startling vision.

The messengers make good time from Caesarea, and by noon the next day are approaching the outskirts of Joppa (verse 9a). As this happens, Peter is making his way on to the roof of the house (looking for shade and the cool of the sea-breeze?) to pray (verse 9b). He is extremely hungry and while lunch is being made for him he falls into some kind of trance (verse 10). Luke calls what he experiences a 'vision' (as with Cornelius, verse 3), though it is difficult to know if he is dreaming, day-dreaming or put in some kind of 'unearthly state' by God. Whichever it is, Peter 'sees' a sheet with animals in it (some of them banned by Jewish law, Lev. 11 verses 1–47) which he is told to eat (verses 11–13). God tells him that God has made these animals clean so he can eat them (verse 15). This happens three times (verse 16).

Peter is confused by this vision, but God has the messengers from Cornelius outside to help unravel the mystery. Peter is to leave the roof and respond positively to their request to go to Cornelius (verse 20). He identifies himself and asks what these travellers want (verse 21). The men describe their master and explain about the vision Cornelius has had. They hope Peter will be persuaded by his character and by his good standing among Jews, to come with them. If not, they hope he will be convinced by the story of an angel visiting their master, despite the fact that he is a Gentile (verse 22). As it happens, Peter has already been instructed to do this by an even higher authority than Cornelius (verse 20)! Peter (presumably with Simon's permission!) invites the travellers into the house for food, refreshment and a good night's sleep after their journey up the coast (verse 23).

For Peter, the meaning of the vision is slowly becoming clear. It was not really about what food he could eat or who he could eat it with; it was a vision of far deeper significance. How deep, he could not have realised at this point. All his pre-conceptions about God's plan and purpose with regard to the Gentiles was about to radically change. And this shift in his thinking came not by his human wisdom or initiative nor by some strategic mission plan thought up by the apostles. This is God's work and Luke is at pains to highlight the supernatural aspects of change of heart which opened up the Gentile mission field (verses 3,11,19, etc.).

Questions

1. *Does God still speak through angel visits (verse 3) and 'trances' (verse 10)? Why are these forms of guidance so rare?*

2. *Do you think Christians have traditions and customs (see verses 12–14) that have grown up over the years? What are they? Do they put people off the church?*

3. *Hospitality plays a large part in these verses (9:43; 10:23). How can we develop this gift in the life of our church?*

Acts 10:23b-33

Peter and Cornelius Together

Peter travels to meet Cornelius in Caesarea. The barrier with the Gentiles is being broken down as the two men meet and share what brought them together.

After a good night's rest (though for Peter it may have been filled with unanswered questions, and no doubt, some more prayer!) the group of ten (see 11:12) set off for Caesarea (verse 23b). The thirty mile journey takes a little longer going back and the group do not arrive until the next day.

Cornelius is ready for them, and has assembled quite a crowd of his family members and friends (verse 24). He obviously senses that this is an occasion of great significance and wants to share it with those close to him. Peter arrives, and Cornelius bows in deep reverence to him (verse 25 – not simply a mark of respect, more like 'worship'). Peter is not used to this treatment (he may have thought it close to idolatry) and encourages Cornelius to stand up (verse 26 cf. Rev. 19:9,10). The instruction to summon Peter to come may have been supernatural, but Peter is only too aware of his humanness – 'I am only a man' – reverence of this kind belongs only to God.

Going inside Peter finds a large (verse 27) and expectant congregation. 'I shouldn't really be here', he admits, 'but I've had a vision which told me God's assessment of people was more important than mine. I have come in obedience to Him, without raising any of the usual objections a Jew would raise in these circumstances. How can I help you?' (verses 28,29).

This really was a remarkable speech from a first century Jew. It shows how much the vision (verses 11–16) was altering his viewpoint and how he is beginning to grasp its significance.

Cornelius then explains how the invitation to Peter came about (verses 30–32); Peter has heard most of this from the messengers (verses 22,23) but the repetition no doubt helps fill in some of the details and also ensures that everyone in the large gathering knows the background to the meeting. Cornelius thanks Peter for coming (verse 33a) and expresses the belief that God is present in the room, that He wants to speak, that He wants to speak through Peter and that the assembled crowd is ready to listen (verse 33b).

This speech is almost as remarkable as Peter's! A Roman military leader speaking to a Jew (in front of witnesses) in such a humble way, is amazing. He shows outstanding spiritual insight and openness.

Questions

1. Cornelius gets family and friends together to hear the gospel (verse 24) and he isn't even a Christian! How can we communicate the gospel better to our friends and families? (Using our homes?)

2. 'Worshipping' Peter is wrong (verse 25). Is it possible to hero-worship a Christian leader too much? Or a church history character? Or a Christian musician?

3. Humility is a key feature in both what Peter says (verses 28,29) and in what Cornelius says (verses 30–32). Why is humility important? How can it be encouraged and developed?

Acts 10:34–48

The Gentiles Believe!

Peter preaches an evangelistic message to the assembled Gentiles. There is an amazing response. A new phase in the life of the early church begins.

Peter opens his sermon with a confession (verse 34), admitting how he has come to realise his mistaken thinking about the Gentiles. 'God has no favourites' is a total climb-down for a Jew, who had probably been brought up to believe that he was part of God's favourite nation. (The Jews were a 'chosen' people, of course; but this was not meant to imply a special *status*, simply a special *opportunity*, that through them the nations of the world could be blessed). God could accept people irrespective of their place of birth or nationality.

The 'meat' of Peter's sermon (verses 36–43) contains many of the same elements he has used before (2:14f, 3:11f). These repeated themes (for example 'Jesus is God's chosen Messiah', 'we are the witness', etc.) form the foundation of apostolic preaching over these early years. They are a presentation of historical facts with an invitation to respond to their implications. That is, if Jesus really did do all these things and He really is alive (and the apostles have seen this with their own eyes, see 1 John 1:1,2); if He is the unique chosen one, the only 'logical' response is to believe and follow Him.

This sermon of Peter's laid more stress than some of his others on the life and ministry of Jesus (verses 37,38). Perhaps a Gentile congregation in Caesarea needed more reminding about this than the Jews in Jerusalem.

The ministry of Jesus occurred in a very small geographical area (his trip to Egypt as a baby may have been the farthest he ever went, Matt. 2:13) and it would have been a mistake to assume that some in this Gentile audience knew any more about Jesus than the haziest of details.

Peter's sermon ends (verse 43 cf. 2:38) with the beginnings of an appeal, but he appears to be interrupted by the Holy Spirit! ('While Peter was *still speaking*' verse 44). The six Jewish Christians can hardly believe their eyes and ears (verse 45); the theory of Peter's sermon ('God has no favourites') is dramatically put into practice – the Holy Spirit is poured out on these Gentiles, just as on them (verse 47). There is no reason to prohibit baptism (into both Christ and the Christian community). Peter stays on for a few days to express commitment to them and no doubt continues the discipleship process (verse 48).

Questions

1. *'Tongues' (verse 46) is a common (though not universal) sign of the work of the Spirit in Acts. Why is this? What emphasis should we give this gift today?*

2. *What could preachers of sermons learn from Peter's preaching content? When is repetition helpful? When is it boring?*

3. *'God has no favourites' (verse 34), but what about the church? Do you get treated better if you are from the south? White? Intelligent? Male? How do we defeat prejudice?*

Acts 11:1–10

Peter in Hot Water

Peter goes from the 'mountain top' of Gentile conversions to the 'valley' of criticism from his peers. He begins to explain the circumstances which led to Gentile contact.

News of the amazing events in Caesarea seem to have reached Jerusalem before Peter did (verse 1). Unlike the modern world, information travelled slowly. It was communicated as quickly as a man could walk (or ride) to the required destination. It could have taken well over a week for anyone in the Capital to hear of these events on the coast, and even then the details may have been 'sketchy'. Peter may have taken several weeks to stay in Caesarea, preach at various towns on the way, and eventually arrive in Jerusalem.

They were waiting impatiently! When he arrived, to a storm of protest from his colleagues (verse 2), he was immediately called on to explain his actions (verse 3). The leadership of the church were clearly 'rattled' by what they had heard. Christians were enjoying a lull in hostilities with the Jewish authorities (9:31) but this kind of activity was bound to provoke outrage and further persecution. Worse still, Peter was seen as leader of the group, so they would all be tainted by his behaviour.

This incident shows how strongly the Jewish culture and perspective still had a grip on hearts and minds in this period of the church's development. Stephen had pointed away from the traditional elements of Judaism (7:2–53 – The Law, the Land, the Temple) to the arrival of the Messiah. Philip had taken the gospel to half-Jews (the Samaritans – 8:1) and the break with the past continues. Peter is about to push the whole church into a radical step away from its past and into its future!

Peter's defence consists of telling his fellow-leaders *exactly* what happened (verse 4). News would have arrived from various sources and in the weeks before he came back to Jerusalem, rumours would have been rife. Peter wants the issue discussed on the basis of the *facts*. So he recounts precisely what happened to him in Joppa, at Simon's house (verses 5–10 cf. 10:9–16).

We have now read this account twice. Luke records the details for us on both occasions (rather than in this passage, just giving us a summary of the previous account). It is such a crucial issue, he even repeats the main point – 'Do not call unclean, what God has called clean' – three times! (10:15, 28; 11:9)

Questions

1. *Why is 'rumour' still so common in church life: Why do we criticise (verse 2) without checking our facts?*

2. *Change threatened these leaders (verse 3). Why do we find change so difficult? How can we become less defensive?*

3. *Peter had changed his mind about the Gentiles (verse 9). Do we admit when we are wrong? Are we open to the possibility that we might be wrong? Why do we find this difficult?*

Acts 11:11–18

Peter Convinces the Christians

Peter continues his defence by explaining what happened after the vision. The power of God on the Gentiles opens the door for their acceptance.

Verse eleven sees Peter warming to his theme, as he recounts the amazing events at Caesarea (cf. 10:17–47). By repeating this information in detail Luke continues to stress the importance of the issue. It is not Peter who is on trial, but the whole future of Christianity. A rejection of what Peter has done will condemn the Christian message to the backwaters of history, as a variation of Judaism. An acceptance will do nothing less than open Christianity up to the world!

Peter has brought the six members of the church in Joppa, who went with him to Caesarea, back to Jerusalem (verse 12b). He must have known that his actions would cause uproar, so he brings them to give supporting eye-witness evidence ... not to mention moral support!

You can almost hear the excitement in Peter's voice as the story is re-told; even he can hardly believe it really happened. He reminds them of what Jesus said, just before His ascension (verse 16 cf. 1:5) about the Holy Spirit. 'If God accepted these Gentiles' Peter argues, 'How could I do anything else but accept them too. I couldn't possibly go against what God was saying' (verse 17).

Peter's case can be summarised as follows: 'God took the initiative, God arranged the circumstances, God poured out His Spirit ... what would you have done in my situation'. On hearing this they withdraw their accusations and consider their questions answered (verse 18a). And this is no grudging acceptance of Peter's account. There is genuine delight at this evidence of divine activity – they 'praised God'. Even those 'unclean' Gentiles have found favour with God (verse 18b). The phrase '*even* the Gentiles' sounds patronising to our ears, even arrogant. But we have to remember the huge gulf which existed between Jews and Gentiles. In the light of this, verse eighteen is an earth-shaking admission!

We can see that Luke intends us to understand that the Gentiles receive spiritual life on the same basis as the Jews – repentance. In Acts, repentance is seen as the key which unlocks the door into God's blessing (2:38; 3:19; 5:31; verse 18). We would do well to remember this crucial emphasis. A casual 'accepting Jesus as Saviour' is no substitute for genuine repentance and faith. Spiritual power flows only from the latter!

Questions

1. Do you 'praise God' (verse 18a) when people you disagree with get blessed? Why is this so difficult for us?

2. God takes the initiative throughout this passage. How can we make sure that we let His ideas affect church life, not just our plans and ideas?

3. Why is repentance (verse 18b) stressed so little in church life today? Why is it important? What difference would it make to, for example, our relationships with other Christians?

Acts 11:19–24

The Church Expands

The message of the Good News spread to more and more people, further and further away from Jerusalem. Barnabas is sent to monitor the situation and encourage.

The ripples from Stephen's death (8:1) continue outwards. Phoenicia was an area along the Mediterranean coast, starting forty miles north of Caesarea and continuing over a hundred and fifty miles to the north. Cyprus is only accessible by boat, over 250 miles from Jerusalem; Antioch was about 300 miles north of Jerusalem (verse 19). These distances begin to illustrate how fast the church is growing and how quickly the message is spreading. The bad news of Stephen's death has turned into good news for the transmitting of the gospel. Because news of the 'Cornelius decision' (11:18) had not reached this far, the message was still aimed at Jews (verse 19b). There were exceptions to this (verse 20) and no doubt Greeks were an obvious target group because of the common language. (Notice that missionaries had come from Cyrene to preach. Cyrene is on the north African coast about *1,000* miles from Jerusalem! Christianity is no longer a local operation. God obviously blessed this missionary activity because many people became Christians (verse 21).

News eventually reached the apostles (many weeks later?), who wanted to make sure things were being done decently and in order. They would also want to ensure that good foundations were laid and proper structures established – so Barnabas is sent to Antioch (verse 22 cf. 8:14). What he finds is a genuine work of God which thrills him (verse 33a). He will be able to take a positive report back to base. His only instruction is about remaining 'true to the Lord' (verse 23b). This seems a slightly odd phrase – no other group of converts has been told this in Acts – until we remember the context – Antioch. This was a thriving mega-city of half a million population, the third largest in the Roman empire. It was a sophisticated city of culture, with dozens of racial groupings, nationalities, religions and lifestyles mingling together. It was known as a city of vice, almost any perversion could be 'enjoyed' – at a price. Barnabas is keen to keep the new converts 'true' in the face of so many temptations and pressures.

The passage concludes with a glowing tribute to Barnabas (verse 24, a similar description to Stephen, 6:5). The apostles could not have sent a better man – Spirit-filled, full of faith, good ... and an effective evangelist (verse 24b)!

Questions

1. How can we help new converts remain 'true to the Lord' (verse 23)? Why do so many slip away from God and the church?

2. Verse 24 is a great tribute to Barnabas. How would you like to be described? How are you described?

3. How can we encourage our church to think in terms of the world, not just our own locality? Why is there a tendency to be inward looking?

Acts 11:25–30

Barnabas and Saul

Barnabas renews his contact with Saul and together they work in Antioch. After a prophetic warning of famine, money is sent to the Jerusalem leadership to help.

Barnabas, sensing the strategic importance of Antioch, decides to stay and continue ministry there. But he is aware of the size of the task and remembers that Saul is in his home town of Tarsus (9:30) about 150 miles away. He sets off to find him (verse 25) and brings him back to Antioch. Out of their friendship, begun many months earlier (9:27), a ministry team develops. For a year they engage in vigorous evangelism and discipleship (verse 26a) very effectively.

Soon, enough people have responded to the Good News to arouse the attention of the sophisticated population of Antioch, who gave them a nickname, 'Christians' (verse 26b). Initially, this was no doubt intended as a term of ridicule, but it quickly caught on. The believers themselves soon saw how appropriate the name was and it stuck (cf. 1 Peter 4:16).

As the year of ministry went on, Barnabas and Saul were joined by a group of prophets from Jerusalem (verse 27). Agabus predicts famine on a massive scale (verse 28) and Luke (writing some time later) adds his own note to tell us how accurate this prophecy was. The Jerusalem disciples, as a harassed minority, would fare particularly badly in famine; with this in mind a collection is taken up among their less-harassed (probably wealthier) fellow believers (verse 29). They sent the gift with Barnabas and Saul, to the leaders back in Judea (verse 30) – the newest disciples giving generously to support the parent-church in its need.

The story of the church at Antioch signals a shift in power away from Jerusalem. Less of the story in Acts will focus on Judea, more on the world beyond its borders; Paul is featured more than Peter; and the base for operations of missionary activity is Antioch, just as much as Jerusalem. The child is out-growing the parent and all the problems of dealing with adolescence are going to hit the headquarters of established Christianity very soon.

Not only is all this going on, but even the adoption of the name 'Christian' is rapidly distinguishing the believers from Judaism, and to some extent separating them from it. Ties with the past are being cut, rapid expansion makes control difficult – the church is on a roller-coaster of change.

Questions

1. *What an amazing prophecy (verse 28)! Is the gift of prophecy for today? What is it for?*

2. *How do we react when we lose power or prestige? What is our attitude to those who take our place (cf. John 3:30)?*

3. *What nickname would you give your church? Or the 'Christians' in your house group? How can we live up to our original 'nickname (verse 27)?*

Acts 12:1–10

Peter's Miraculous Escape

Peter, back in Jerusalem after his travels, is an obvious target for Herod. He is arrested and imprisoned but God arranges a supernatural escape.

For some reason Herod decides that now is the time to persecute the church (verse 1) more vigorously. He was not a popular character, indeed his whole family had been hated by the Jews. Because of this he seems to bend over backwards to please the Jews; his offensive against the church may be part of his desire to keep in with the Jewish establishment. Anyway, he arrests James on some trumped up charge, and has him beheaded (verse 2). This so delights the Jews that Herod decides to pick up the top man (verse 3a) and have him thrown in prison. Unfortunately for Herod the 'show trial' will have to be delayed because no public hearing was possible during the period of Passover.

This was the anniversary of the death of Jesus and Peter may well have thought that he was going to die at the same Jewish feast as his Master, perhaps by the same method! Herod is anxious not to lose his prize exhibit, so he assigns sixteen soldiers to guard him, in groups of four, round the clock (verse 4). Peter is not going to escape this time (cf. 5:19)!

But the church was praying (verse 5). Luke consistently emphasises prayer in Acts and its mention here is yet another reminder of the divine dimension. Peter's fate is not at the whim of Herod the Jew-pleaser or the Jewish authorities. Above the power politics and clamouring for approval, a higher force is at work; actually, a higher person is at work. At just the right time, the night before the trial (verse 6) God intervenes. Peter is sleeping (which shows he had an amazing sense of peace) and has to be jolted awake by the angel (12:7). Despite the fact that he is chained between two soldiers, and there are two more guarding him (verse 6), Peter gets up, puts his shoes and outer clothes on, and follows the angel (verse 8). He follows the angel half-asleep, half-mesmerised, wondering if this is a dream or a vision (verse 9). No, it is really happening; those guards they are passing are real enough (are the guards asleep? drunk? in a trance?) as is the iron gate (verse 10), which opens 'automatically'. After a few moments of freedom the angel leaves as suddenly as he had arrived (verse 10b). Despite Herod's precautions, Peter is free.

Questions

1. James is killed (verse 2) but Peter is set free (verse 7f). Did God like Peter more than James? How can we explain this? Or is it just a mystery?

2. Herod wants to please the Jews. How does who you want to please affect your behaviour? Who should we want to please most (cf. Col. 1:10)?

3. A praying church (verse 5). How can we become a church like this? Why are prayer meetings usually so poorly attended?

Acts 12:11–19a

Peter – An Answered Prayer

Peter makes his way to the prayer meeting ... and can't get in! They respond to Peter's escape with astonishment; Herod responds with anger.

Peter pinches himself a few times to make sure all this is really happening (verse 11) and it dawns on him just how amazing his escape has been. Herod has been evaded and the Jewish leaders disappointed (verse 11b), and it is God who has done it. Realising how dangerous it is for him to be out on the streets at night, he hurries to a home where
Christians live (a young John Mark lives here; later to go with Paul on a missionary journey and write the second gospel) and discovers a prayer meeting going on (verse 12)!

It is a sizable home and Peter is forced to knock loudly on a locked outer door until Rhoda goes to the door (verse 13). He tells her who he is and she races back to the prayer meeting (forgetting to let Peter in!) with the amazing news (verse 14). This whole scene is the stuff of 'farce' and comedy – no doubt evoking gales of laughter as it was retold throughout the Christian community. 'Peter is at the door', 'O no he isn't', 'O yes he is' ... and so on! The intensity of the prayer had made Rhoda hallucinate or his angel was paying them a visit (verse 15). All this time, a very real, very frustrated Peter is trying to get off the street out of danger, into the security of the house (verse 16).

Perhaps they were not expecting an answer so quickly or in quite this way; but they were totally flabbergasted. At last they let Peter in and eventually settled down enough to hear his story (verse 17a). Once the story was told he asked that James (the brother of Jesus – emerging more and more as a leader in the Jerusalem church) and the other leaders be informed. He then left (presumably getting out more easily than he got in!) to go to 'another place' (verse 17b). This was probably to a Christian 'safe house' in the Jerusalem area, and then much farther away; perhaps back to Simon's house in Joppa, or more likely, completely out of Herod's clutches to Antioch, or even to Rome.

If there was a commotion at Mark's house in the night, there was an even greater one at the prison the next morning (verse 18)! Everyone is confused and bewildered. Herod, having lost his means of gaining the applause of the Jewish leaders, is in no mood for mercy. Peter's guards are condemned to death (verse 19).

Questions

1. *How do we respond when God answers prayer in ways we do not expect (verse 16)? How do we respond when He does not seem to answer at all?*

2. *Has God got a sense of humour? What do you think He finds funny? Should we laugh more in church?*

3. *Herod is angry and cruel (verse 19). How do we handle our anger? What kind of things are said and done because of anger? How can we learn to control our tempers?*

Acts 12:19b–24

Herod Dies

Some internal political problems distract Herod from persecuting the Church. His death is a reminder of God's authority. The Church continues growing.

Herod had a sizable administrative and military task, so affairs of state would have to take priority over keeping well in with Jewish leaders. Besides, he may have found Jerusalem a little claustrophobic for someone used to the freedoms of Rome. Anyway, he goes away from the capital to the coast at Caesarea (verse 19b). Tyre and Sidon are Mediterranean ports about 60 and 85 miles (respectively) north of Caesarea in Phoenicia. There would have been fierce competition for trade between Caesarea and the two Phoenician ports, and this could have been the source of the friction with Herod (verse 20). Whatever the cause, the Phoenicians decided to work together and get Herod to the negotiating table. They desperately needed his goodwill because their food supply came largely from Galilee. A personal and trusted servant (and advisor?) helped set up the meeting (verse 20).

Once the day arrives, Herod treats the occasion more like a coronation than a discussion. Dressed in opulent splendour, seated on a throne, he pompously addresses his subjects ((verse 21) and the visiting Phoenicians?). The response to his speech is grovelling flattery (verse 22) – either from his cringing courtiers or from manipulative Phoenicians (or both!). Herod foolishly accepts their acclaim, only to be immediately reminded by God that he is not a god, but a very mortal human – he is struck dead (verse 23)! (There has been a lot of speculation about how Herod died. He seems to have been struck with an abdominal or intestinal complaint. A number of round worms could block internal tubes, ultimately causing death.)

Whatever the physical cause of death, Luke clearly understands it to be an Act of God. The obvious, stated reason for his death is idolatry – he applied to himself what is meant for God alone. He may also be being punished for his persecution of the church. Later Christians would have drawn comfort from this passage as they faced Roman persecution. Many had to give praise to Caesar as a god or die. Herod 'did not give praise to God (verse 23)' and he died. Their God really is greater than Caesar!

And the gospel goes on flourishing (verse 24). Roman kings may come and go (verse 23), political squabbles may dominate things for a while (verse 20) ... but the 'word of God' outlasts them all! (verse 24 cf. 1 Peter 1:24,25).

Questions

1. *What is the difference between flattery and praise? Why does flattery diminish the giver and receiver (verse 22)?*

2. *Why is pride so dangerous (verse 23)? How can we spot it in ourselves? How can we work to prevent it (see Phil. 2:3–11)?*

3. *What kinds of things last? Why are we so obsessed with things which will rot/rust/wear out? How can we transfer our priorities from the passing to the permanent (Isaiah 40:6–8; Heb. 13:8)?*

Acts 12:25 – 13:3

Barnabas and Saul Commissioned

After spending time in Jerusalem, Barnabas and Saul return to Antioch. Their call to missionary work is supernaturally confirmed and they are sent out.

Barnabas and Saul were sent from Antioch with money for the Jewish Christians (11:30). Having done this, they recruit John Mark (the cousin of Barnabas (Col. 4:10)) and return to Antioch (verse 25).

Luke then lists five key leaders in the Antioch church, describing them as prophets and teachers. (Some of the prophets may have been part of the prophetic team from Jerusalem (11:27). These leaders may have had a travelling ministry, but they appear to be based in Antioch, and have some on-going commitment to the church there. Barnabas and Saul are the familiar names in this list (verse 1), but the other three are relatively obscure. Their names indicate both the cosmopolitan nature of Antioch and the diversity of background from which converts to Christianity now came. Simeon is a black man, probably from Africa (some people think he may be 'Simon of Cyrene' who carried the cross for Jesus (Luke 23:26); Lucius was from a north African province and Manaen had political and aristocratic connections.

This diverse quintet provide both the teaching input into the lives of the Christians and the specifically inspirational direction from the Spirit. They may all have had both ministries or (as the original language implies) the first three were prophets and the last two teachers.

Worship and fasting were a regular feature of corporate Christian life (verse 2). On one of these occasions the Holy Spirit instructed (presumably through a prophetic word from one of the prophets) that Barnabas and Saul be commissioned for a special ministry. No doubt this did not come as a surprise to them (Saul, for example, would have been aware of God's purpose for his life; at least in general terms, cf. 9:15) but it would have been a growing confirmation of their sense of call. The exact nature of the call and place of service is not explained; God will direct them at the right time.

After more praying and fasting (the prophetic word would have to be carefully 'tested' (1 Cor. 14:29)) Barnabas and Saul were commissioned by the laying on of hands (verse 3 cf. 6:6 – the commissioning of deacons). After this, they were released from their duties in Antioch and sent out on their mission. Here is a divinely chosen team – a prophet and a teacher – to ensure that the word of God continues to spread (12:24).

Questions

1. *Have you ever fasted? Why/why not? Should the whole church fast before major decisions (see verse 2)?*

2. *Are there any prophets today (see verse 1)? What is a prophetic ministry? What is the gift of prophecy? What is it for?*

3. *How many missionaries has your church sent out? How can we encourage more short-term and long-term missionaries to go out from our congregation (verse 3)?*

Acts 13:4–12

Mission Journey Number One Begins

Barnabas and Saul (who becomes Paul) set off on their missionary travels. Opposition from a false prophet is overcome and a leading citizen is converted.

Barnabas and Saul travelled the sixteen mile journey west to Seleucia (verse 4) and from there sailed to Cyprus. Barnabas was from Cyprus (4:36) so he could show Saul around and introduce him to some of the key people on the island. They land at the major administrative centre of Salamis on the east coast (verse 5) and begin to preach and teach. Mark is a 'helper'; he may have carried the bags as a servant or been involved in some of the discipling of new converts – or both.

After an island-wide evangelistic tour, they arrive in Paphos, the capital (verse 6a). Here they meet a 'Jewish sorcerer' (strictly speaking a contradiction in terms – like a 'Christian thief' – sorcery was officially banned in Judaism) who was an attendant at the court of the island's ruler, Sergius Paulus (verses 6b,7a). The proconsul wants to hear about this strange deviation from Judaism and has Barnabas and Saul brought before him (verse 7b). He is a wise and thoughtful man who may have had some openness to Jewish ideas. Certainly with such a large Jewish population under his authority he would have been aware of their teaching and customs.

Elymas, with his strange mixture of Jewish belief and occult involvement, tries to interrupt Saul's presentation of the gospel (verse 8). Saul confronts him with a dramatic accusation about the source of his power (the devil), the wickedness of his life and the manipulative nature of his actions (verse 10)! God will strike him physically blind (an illustration of his spiritual blindness) for a time (verse 11a) – and Elymas is struck immediately (verse 11b). This incident is very similar to Philip's experience, as he takes the gospel to Samaria. He encounters Simon the sorcerer and demonstrates the greater power of God (8:9f). Paul encounters Elymas the sorcerer and demonstrates the same power of God. New areas of missionary activity do seem to provoke power-encounters of this kind (cf. 16:16).

Sergius Paulus is convinced by this demonstration of spiritual authority (verse 12a) and the quality of the teaching he hears about Jesus (verse 12b). Notice that he is amazed at the 'teaching' not the miracle. Signs of supernatural activity do not seem to have been uncommon in the ancient world; clear, uncompromising teaching may have been rarer! Belief in Jesus was obviously based on a rational response to a series of facts – confirmed by a miraculous sign.

Questions

1. *The Devil is active today (verse 10 cf. 1 Peter 5:8). How can he be recognised and defeated? Where does 'spiritual warfare' fit in?*

2. *Paul does not seem to have been polite to Elymas (verse 10f)! Are Christians today too nice? Why are we afraid to be blunt and direct?*

3. *Good teaching is important (verse 12b). What is 'good teaching' for today? How can we increase our knowledge of Biblical books and Christian doctrine?*

Acts 13:13–25

Paul – A Synagogue Sermon

Paul and Barnabas leave Cyprus and travel to the mainland. They are invited to speak in a synagogue, where Paul explains the Old Testament background to Christianity.

From Cyprus the missionary party travel north to Perga in Asia Minor. Here John Mark leaves them (verse 13), and returns to Jerusalem. Something serious seems to have provoked this departure. It was over 1,000 miles by land back to Jerusalem (or 600 miles by sea, via Cyprus) – not a journey you would undertake without very good reason. Perhaps Mark is concerned that Saul is increasingly using his Roman name (Paul) and ministering to the Gentiles; he may have resented Paul's taking over the leadership of the group from his cousin Barnabas. Paul saw Mark's leaving as simple desertion, a dereliction of duty (15:38).

From Perga they went 100 miles north to Antioch in Pisidia (verse 14) where they were invited to speak in the synagogue – quite an honour for these Christian travellers. (Perhaps the synagogue rulers were vaguely sympathetic, genuinely interested or just imagined Saul and Barnabas were good orthodox Jews visiting from Jerusalem!) Saul stands up and begins his first recorded speech in Acts (verse 16). The content of the sermon has similarities with Stephen's to the Sanhedrin (7:2–53).

Paul describes the powerful hand of God at work in one major strand of Jewish thinking – the provision of the Land. This Land was kept for them while they were in Egypt (verse 17), and while they grumbled in the desert (verse 18); God kicked out the Canaanites from the Land (verse 19) and provided a succession of judges and a king (verse 20) until David arrived. This man was approved by God (verse 22) and was the human dynasty through which God chose to reveal His Messiah (verse 23). The Land is important because it provides a context for the Messiah to be born into and shows God's faithfulness to what He promised; but the Messiah is the crucial part of the revelation!

Jesus is God's Messiah, the Saviour (verse 23, cf. Matt. 1:21) and was introduced to the Jews through the last of the Old Testament-style prophets, John the Baptist (verse 24). John is quite clear that he is not the Messiah (verse 25a). But with brutal honesty and a total lack of pride, he explains that he is not even worthy to be Messiah's slave, the one who helps take his Master's shoes off (verse 25b, cf. Matt. 3:11)! He, like others before him, simply points the way.

Questions

1. *Christians sometimes fall out (verse 13)! How do we treat people we have fallen out with? How can we bring about reconciliation?*

2. *Jews were sometimes so focussed on a good thing (the Land) they missed the best thing (the Messiah). In what ways can the good things become bad, or are used for wrong purposes?*

3. *Mark may have been jealous of Paul's growing prestige. What kinds of people are you jealous of? What provokes jealousy in you? How can it be dealt with?*

Acts 13:26–41

Paul's Sermon Continues

Paul moves into the explanation section of his sermon, by focussing on Jesus. His death and resurrection are described, concluding with the offer of forgiveness.

Paul starts the second phase of his speech with a similar phrase to his opening (verse 26 cf. verse 16); he identifies Jews and Jewish converts or God-fearers in his congregation. This section of the sermon finds echoes in Paul's letters (1 Cor. 15:3–5) and is a repetition of some of the main features of Peter's earlier sermons (e.g. Jewish leaders responsible for Jesus' death, verses 27,28 cf. 4:10). Apostles were witnesses to the resurrection (verse 31 cf. 2:32). This reminds Luke's readers of the core material at the heart of early Christian preaching and the commitment to these facts by both Peter and Paul – the two characters who emerge as the most influential in the first period of Christian development.

This similarity with Peter's material is most striking in the section which points away from David (the great Jewish hero) to his 'successor' Jesus, who has been prophetically foretold (verse 32 cf. Psalm 2:7). David stayed dead so Psalm 16:10 (verse 35) cannot apply to him, it must apply to someone else. That 'someone else' is Jesus, who is not dead but alive! (verses 35–37 cf. Peter in 2:27–31 where the argument is identical.)

Paul is impressive because he can not only articulate the historical facts clearly but he can interpret their *significance* and apply it both corporately and personally. This remarkable ability (seen supremely in Jesus, Matt

7:29) was absent in most of the teachers of the law, who knew the minutiae of the Scriptures but not what their purpose was. Paul, on the other hand, knows the content of Jewish law and history (even if he is a bit hazy about where two of his quotations come from! verse 34 – Isaiah 55:3,35; Psalm 16:10) and has the wisdom and divinely given insight to apply it.

The sermon ends with a gentle appeal ('brothers' verse 38) that only through Jesus can anyone be forgiven of their sins (verse 38 cf. 2:38) 'Everyone who believes' (verse 39) is a remarkable statement to make in a Jewish synagogue; it suddenly opens up the door to the residents of a planet rather than the people of a single nation. The gentle appeal is followed up by a warning, taken from Habakkuk 1:5: 'Watch out those who mock this message, they are finished. God is doing something so wonderful, so mind-blowing, you just can't comprehend it' (verse 41). 'Take care' (verse 40) says Paul, don't miss out on what God is doing.

Questions

1. *What do you think is the basic core-material of our faith? Which ten subjects would you cover in a discipleship course for new Christians?*

2. *Can you list the Old Testament books in order? Do you know the main points of each of the minor prophets? Do facts like this matter or is the overall meaning the important thing?*

3. *Jesus has defeated death (verses 34,37). How should this fact affect our view of death? Why are we so often afraid of it?*

Acts 13:42–52

Responses to the Gospel

Paul and Barnabas continue to answer questions and present the gospel to any who will listen. The message produces both conversions and persecution.

Paul and Barnabas leave the synagogue and appear to be well received; at least people seem open minded enough to hear more from them on the following Saturday (verse 42). A sizable group seem to have been caught up in the excitement of the message, and are urged on by the two visitors to continue being faithful to the teaching they have heard (verse 43). Both the element of human responsibility ('continue') and the element of divine activity ('grace') are stressed here. Life in the kingdom is a partnership with God. We are not free to abdicate all responsibility for our spiritual lives to God, neither are we condemned to carry the burden alone – He provides His grace, we commit ourselves to living in its power.

After a week of great anticipation, a huge crowd gathers to hear Paul and Barnabas (verse 44). The sheer size of the crowd produces envy in the Jewish leaders; things are getting out of hand, they are in danger of losing their status and influence. They hurl insults at Paul, mocking what he is teaching (verse 45) and this despite Paul's warning about such behaviour (verses 40,41!). Paul and Barnabas are forced to respond to this attack by explaining that if they don't want to respond to the Good News they will go direct to the Gentiles. God has used Isaiah 49:6 to call them to the Gentiles, and they are not going to be disobedient (verses 46,47).

These statements become the operational method for Paul and his mission team – first to the Jews, then to the Gentiles (cf. Rom. 1:16). He adopts this policy in all the cities he visits.

The crowd of Gentiles in Antioch were delighted, and many were converted, as God worked in their lives (verse 48). The gospel even got out into the district around Antioch (verse 49), but their success was not without cost. Civic leaders, and others in authority, were encouraged to see Paul and Barnabas as trouble makers (verse 50a). They were thrown out of the town and driven away from the district completely (verse 50b). In a typically Jewish protest – gesture of scorn – they distanced themselves emotionally and spiritually from their persecutors (verse 51). They also distanced themselves physically by travelling the eighty miles south-east to Iconium. The disciples left behind were far from discouraged – the Holy Spirit had given them a supernatural joy (verse 52).

Questions

1. *What happens to our Christian lives when we try to do things in our own strength? And when we don't try at all?*

2. *Some groups of people are more responsive than others to the gospel (see verse 46). What kinds of people in your community are most open to Jesus? How can they be reached?*

3. *Would you have been filled with joy (verse 52) with all the trouble in Antioch? What produces joy like this? How is joy different from happiness?*

Opponents of the Gospel

As the Good News was preached in the first century world it met resistance in a number of different ways. The sophisticated intellectuals (e.g. Agrippa and the Athens' council) enjoyed discussion but shied away from personal commitment. The deeply religious Jews (e.g. 13:45, 26:22) were jealous of the Christians and unwilling to take the next step of faith – from God to Jesus, His Son.

The worldly-wise cynics (e.g. Felix) were simply not interested in Truth, but wanted to use Christianity for their own ends. The greedy materialists were angry when their wealth was threatened (16:19, 19:25-27) and the

Satan-inspired occultists (e.g. Simon and Elymas) wanted to manipulate the message and its power for their own ends.

This opposition was countered by the power of the Spirit and the teaching of the Word (e.g. 13:6-12). We face similar opposition today, but have access to the same weapons of the Word and the Spirit.

Acts 14:1–7

Preaching in Iconium

Having been expelled from Antioch, Paul and Barnabas begin preaching in Iconium. Teaching and miracles go hand in hand until persecution drives them on again.

When they arrived in Iconium they made their way to the synagogue as was their habit in a new situation (verse 1 cf. 13:5,14). The Good News was so convincingly explained that a large number of both Jews and Gentiles believed (verse 1b). The mention of the Gentiles so early on in the ministry at Iconium is a reminder of the growing focus on them in this missionary enterprise. The Jews may be contacted first, but the Gentiles are not second in any way which diminishes their value as people or their equal right to hear and respond to the gospel.

But as usual trouble is just around the corner, following what is becoming a familiar pattern! (Notice how similar Antioch and Iconium are in this respect: initial interest and response (13:44 cf. verse 1); angry stirrers of trouble (13:50 cf. verse 2); persecution and leaving (13:50 cf. verses 5,6).) Despite the pressure the mission team remain in the town for 'a considerable time' (verse 3) – perhaps several months – preaching with courage a message which God is pleased to honour with amazing demonstrations of power. (These 'signs and wonders' would probably be miracles related to sickness and releasing the demonised.)

Rival viewpoints were expressed all over the city; no doubt one of the main talking points of the day was whose side you were on in the apostles versus Jews debate. Opinion was divided (verse 4). The hostile element (with a little encouragement from their leaders!) decided to stone them. This was not the formal punishment a synagogue might impose (cf. 7:58), more of an illegal lynch-mob involved in a deadly mugging attempt (verse 5). It was time to move on. This time just forty miles to the south west, to a town called Lystra; which was in a different district from Iconium (verse 6). Far from being cowed into silence or driven underground, they continue to tell everyone the message of Good News (verse 7).

These incidents in Antioch and Iconium (and there will be plenty of others throughout Asia Minor) are something of a puzzle to our western twentieth century minds. If Paul and Barnabas spoke in Hyde Park Corner in London or Times Square in New York, it's hard to imagine any response other than some heckling; the vast majority of people would ignore them. But this was a day when what you believed was important, it would affect the way you viewed citizenship and your loyalty to the state. Beliefs were a means of political control – Christians were threatening the very fabric of ancient society!

Questions

1. Do we still have a responsibility to the Jews in terms of evangelism, or is it 'Gentiles first, Jews not at all'? What are some of the pitfalls in Jewish evangelism? How can we get involved?

2. Some minds in this story were 'poisoned' (verse 2). How does this happen today? (Gossip? Slander? Deceit?) Why do we find it so easy to use our tongues as a poisonous weapon (see James 3:8)?

3. Why don't we threaten the fabric of our society? Why is church life often so tame compared with the Church in Acts? How would you like to have Paul as a member of your church? What difference would it make?!

Acts 14:8–20a

Mission in Lystra

Paul and Barnabas narrowly avoid being worshipped as gods after Paul heals a lame man. But a mob stones Paul, leaving him for dead.

Lystra was populated by a largely uneducated, rural people. There were a few Jews in the city but they seem to have had little influence. There may not even have been a synagogue, so the apostolic team gets straight into street preaching, to anyone who will listen. While Paul was speaking he saw a lame man in the crowd. Luke is at pains to describe the extent of his disability (he has badly damaged feet, he was born this way, and he had never been able to walk (verse 8)) in order that the amazement which follows his healing can be understood. Paul sees a rising of faith in the man and instructs him to get up and walk. He does (verses 9,10)! (This story has many similarities to the healing at the Beautiful Gate (3:4–7)). God's power again breaks through as the gospel is preached in a new setting.

The response is completely unexpected. Of course they are amazed at the power working through Paul and Barnabas, but amazement was the usual response (cf. 3:10). What was not usual was for them to be thought Greek gods (verse 11)! In the unsophisticated, superstitious minds of these Lycaonians this was Zeus (Barnabas) and Hermes (Paul) granting them a special divine visitation (verse 12). It took a while for the apostles to catch on to what was happening because the crowd had lapsed into a local dialect (verse 11). And, of course, a response like this in a largely Jewish crowd (or where Jews had influence) would be unthinkable. As this was the usual scenario, they were totally unprepared for what was happening.

By the time the priest of Zeus arrived with sacrificial bulls, they were beginning to understand (verse 13). This behaviour would have been idolatrous to Jews and Christians; everything in Paul and Barnabas was repulsed by this and they ran among the people, tearing their own clothes as they did so, (A Jewish symbolic action showing distress or remorse. cf. Joel 2:13, 2 Kings 19:1–3) urging them to stop (verse 14)! Paul's briefest recorded sermon follows: 'We are men like you (verse 15), there is only one living God, He is the one who made everything (verse 15b) and has provided rain for your crops (verse 17). We are only His messengers!' The sacrifices are only just avoided (verse 18)!

So fickle is public opinion (if they are not gods they must be imposters!) that the Jews from Iconium and Antioch have little difficulty putting their earlier plan into action (verse 5) – Paul is stoned and left for dead (verse 19) outside the city. Incredibly he recovers and bravely returns to Lystra (verse 20).

Questions

1. Is the superstition (verse 12) in this passage around today? What forms does it take?

2. Idolatry (verse 13) was common in the ancient world. What 'idols' do we worship today? If advertising is a guide, what kind of things do people really want?

3. Loyalty is an important quality. Do we desert our friends when they do things we disagree with? How can we demonstrate loyalty to the leadership of our church?

Acts 14:20b–28

The Return to Antioch

Paul and Barnabas travel to Derbe and then re-visit the towns in Asia Minor, before returning to base at Antioch. This completes the first missionary journey.

After being brutally attacked (verse 19) Paul makes an amazing recovery (verse 20); so amazing that he can set off the next day and begin the seventy mile walk to Derbe. Not only was he a man whom God used powerfully, but he must also have been a strong, determined character to cope with all the physical abuse and emotional pressure he experienced on his travels.

Luke tells us about the church being established in Derbe (verse 21) in the briefest terms, before telling us about Paul retracing his steps. He visits each of the towns where they planted churches, before returning to Antioch in Syria. This seemingly simple section of Acts glides over the incredible courage of Paul and Barnabas. Just to mention the towns where they had been so badly treated (verse 21b), never mind re-visit them, must have sent shivers down their spines! Presumably they entered each city secretly (by night? in disguise?) and limited their ministry to the believers, so minimising the risk of detection. They were motivated in these daring visits by the needs of the new, fledgling churches which they had established. They would only survive with additional teaching and the provision of Godly leadership (elders) to guide them (verse 23). These elders were appointed in a similar manner to Paul and Barnabas for their missionary work – in the context of prayer and fasting (verse 23 cf. 13:2,3).

Luke records two aspects of apostolic teaching in these situations – encouragement to persevere and a warning to expect hardship (verse 22). It's hard to think of more helpful, relevant, pastoral advice. For these infant churches the Christian life is not going to be easy but it is going to be wonderful. (For many modern churches it is easy but it is not very wonderful!)

Journeying south from Antioch they arrive at Perga where they have the opportunity to preach; an opportunity they were not able to enjoy on their first visit (verse 25 cf. 13:13,14). Eight miles away, on the coast at Attalia, they take a boat back to Antioch in Syria where they were commissioned (verse 26 cf. 13:1–3). How thrilled the church must have been to have its missionaries back on furlough, telling how God had revealed Himself, especially to the Gentiles (verse 27). Their long stay was, no doubt, for rest and recovery (perhaps Paul needed some medical attention after the stoning) ... not to mention being spiritually nourished themselves!

Questions

1. *Notice the emphasis on follow-up (verse 21b) in this mission. How can we best follow up our new converts? What do they need most in the early weeks?*

2. *It was very hard to go back to these towns (verse 21). Where is the hardest place for you to be a Christian? (Home? Work?) How can we encourage each other to be bold?*

3. *Paul and Barnabas arrived safely back (verses 26,27). How do we greet missionaries on their return? How can we let them know they are loved while they are away?*

Acts 15:1–11

The Jerusalem Council

The early church is faced with deciding how much of Judaism Gentiles need to practice. Paul and Barnabas go as delegates to a council called to decide the issue.

Antioch in Syria receives some visitors who begin teaching that circumcision is essential for salvation (verse 1). These Jewish Christians from Judea may have heard from Mark about the Gentiles coming to faith in large numbers (13:13) and were anxious to reassert the place of Judaism among all the believers. The teaching about circumcision was not simply about submitting to a physical operation but had implications about their respect for Jewish law as a whole. Paul and Barnabas opposed this vehemently (verse 2) and it is obvious a major disagreement has erupted. Only a full-scale debate can settle the matter, and Paul and Barnabas are sent with a delegation to Jerusalem (verse 2b).

As they travelled they told what God was doing among the Gentiles (gathering support for their case?) and in the course of their 300 mile journey made many churches excited by stories of God's power (verse 3). Their arrival in Jerusalem was warmly welcomed by the church, and a preliminary report of their missionary work was shared (verse 4).

When the Council begins in earnest, representatives of the teachers who had been in Antioch restate their position (verse 5 cf. verse 1). No doubt a variety of views were expressed and then the leadership withdrew to consider the matter (verse 6). 'After much (heated?) discussion' (verse 7) Peter stands up to make a major contribution to the debate. He argues against the 'Pharisee party' Christians (verse 5a) and in favour of Paul and Barnabas. His argument is based on two principles: 1) his own experience and 2) a theological truth – salvation is only through Jesus.

God has already shown His commitment to the Gentiles through Peter's ministry to Cornelius (verses 7b-9 cf. 10:9–48). This incident (though perhaps ten years before) was known to everyone, and had been approved at the time (cf. 11:18). In addition, the message had always been about Jesus and turning to Him as the sole provider of salvation (4:12); to add the Jewish law as a requirement would be a 'yoke' (verse 10) that would result in bondage. Peter ends with the clear assertion that both Jews and Gentiles are 'saved' in exactly the same way – through Jesus (verse 11 cf. John 14:6b). God does not distinguish between Jew and Gentile, shows no favouritism (verse 9 cf. 10:34,35) and accepts everyone on the same basis: faith on their part (verse 9), grace on God's part (verse 11).

Questions

1. *Do we add things to the simple gospel message? What do people need to believe to be part of your church?*

2. *Is Jesus really the only way to God? What about other religions? Or being a nice person? Or doing your best?*

3. *Notice the powerful combination of personal testimony and clear principle (verses 7–11). Why are these so convincing together? What does this tell us about the value of a clear testimony and a good grasp of the arguments in favour of Christianity?*

Acts 15:12–21

The Council Concludes

Peter's speech is followed by testimony from Paul and Barnabas, and a 'summing up' from James. A momentous decision is made – Gentiles are not bound by the Law.

After Peter's crucial speech (verses 7–11) the assembly grows silent (verse 12); the hot debate between various factions settles down, and Barnabas and Paul are allowed to share eye-witness accounts of what God is doing among the Gentiles. The Council heard how the same miraculous power which God had used to confirm His message to the Jews, was also released among the Gentiles (3:2–3 cf. 14:8–10). These accounts and Peter's speech seem to have convinced the Council.

James, by now established as a key leader in the Jerusalem church, and almost certainly acting as chairman of the Council, sums up the situation (verse 13). Obviously, whatever Peter said would be influential and James (calling him by his Hebrew name – 'Simon') affirms the pivotal significance of the Cornelius incident (9:14). In addition, he reminds the Council that the Old Testament saw a place for the Gentiles in God's purposes. He quotes from Amos 9:11–12 to show that God had always intended there to be two distinct (but linked) groups who would share in the blessing the Messiah would bring – restored Jews ('rebuild David's fallen tent' (verse 16)) and 'Gentiles who bear my name' (verse 17).

James gives a précis of the summing up, when he declares that nothing should be done to put obstacles in the way of Gentiles who want to turn to faith. They will not have to embrace Judaism; they may come to God on the same basis as the Jews (verse 19 cf. verse 11). This judgement is a clear affirmation of the ministry of Barnabas and Paul. They must have been delighted!

James goes on to suggest some practical guidelines for Gentile behaviour. These instructions seem to be given *not* to appease the Jewish faction but to ensure harmonious relationships between Jewish and Gentile groups of believers (verse 21). James seems keen that the freedom from the Law that Gentiles now enjoyed did not turn into licence; causing unnecessary offence to their Jewish brothers and sisters. He suggests four things which should be avoided to ensure fellowship between Gentile and Jewish Christians – three relate to food (verse 20)! This was a big issue for Jews, deeply embedded in their culture. What you ate and how you ate it, had major ceremonial and religious implications. Jesus challenged this thinking (Matt. 15:16–20) and Peter's vision also challenges it (10:11–16).

Questions

1. In what ways do we make it difficult in our churches for those who are not Christians (see verse 19)? What do they find difficult about – our services? our premises? our organisations?

2. We smile at the Jewish concerns with food (verse 20) but are we guilty of gluttony? Obsession with dieting? Wasting food?

3. To what extent should we be ready to avoid behaviour which offends others (verses 20,21)? Are there any limits to this?

Acts 15:22–34

Spelling out the Decision

The Council writes down the decision it has come to and sends it with a delegation to Antioch. The letter is well received and the church is encouraged.

It seemed sensible to the Council to convey their feelings on such an important matter in writing and in person. A decision of this kind of significance must be communicated as clearly as possible. Judas and Silas are chosen as representatives of the Jerusalem church, to take the letter and explain its content (verse 22). The letter is intended to be read in Antioch first, but also to Gentile Christians over a much larger area (verse 23 – Antioch, Syria and Cilicia). This is not a small issue where a single group of believers has a problem, and the mother-church responds to it. This is the largest single issue the church has faced in its short history – every Christian congregation will be affected by the Council's decision.

The letter makes it clear that the teachers who provoked the trouble in the first place (verse 1) were not sent or authorised by the Jerusalem church (verse 24). The letter also clearly affirms Paul and Barnabas as people (verse 25 – 'dear friends') and in their ministries (verse 26 'risked their lives'). The decision the letter contains has a divine source combined with their human wisdom (verse 28) – God approves of Gentile mission and so do the Jerusalem Christians! The four guidelines to promote good relationships between Jewish and Gentile believers are spelt out. Notice that these are issues of immense practical importance, not theoretical niceties. For example food offered to idols was a major source of friction and disagreement at Corinth (1 Cor.8f.).

It must not be forgotten that the Jerusalem Council have made a gracious, generous and costly decision for them. Every advance among the Gentiles makes their own situation among Orthodox Jews more difficult. By coming to this decision they have opened themselves up to the probability of ever-increasing persecution in their own country.

The church in Antioch was called together for a special meeting, where the letter was read and explained. Not surprisingly, it was received with great delight (verses 30,31). It was useful to have two such gifted brothers as Judas and Silas in Antioch, and their prophetic ministries were put to good use (verse 32). There was much encouragement – both through the letter (verse 31) and through their ministry (verse 32). Living in this huge centre of vice and other religions they probably needed it!

Silas and Judas eventually return to Jerusalem, taking happy memories and blessings back home (verse 33).

Questions

1. How many of the four guidelines (verse 29) apply today? Explain your answer!
2. Right decisions can be costly decisions. Think of some examples.
3. Encouragement is vital in church life (verses 31, 32). How can we encourage ... the lonely? the pressurised? the leaders? How can we develop a 'ministry of encouragement'?

Acts 15:35–41

The Second Mission Begins

Now that a clear position has been established on Gentile evangelism, Paul and Barnabas are anxious to spread the word still further – separately!

Paul and Barnabas stayed in Antioch with a ministry to both believers ('taught') and non-believers ('preached') – along with an increasing number of people who were developing these ministries (verse 35). Paul was a man born with 'itchy feet'! By Acts 15 he has been in Tarsus, Jerusalem, Damascus, (Arabia), Damascus, Jerusalem, Caesarea, Tarsus, Antioch, 'the first missionary journey', Antioch, Jerusalem and back to Antioch. He suggests to Barnabas that they need to re-visit the churches they have planted (verse 36). Barnabas agrees, but wants to take his cousin Mark with them (verse 37). It is a case of 'once bitten, twice shy' for Paul, who considers Mark a deserter (v. 39 cf. 13:13). Paul appears to doubt his 'stickability' and may still feel personally aggrieved by Mark's attitude.

Paul and Barnabas are unable to reconcile their differences ('a sharp disagreement'!, verse 39) and split up as a mission team. (It is helpful to realise that personality clashes and strong differences of opinion occurred in the early church as well as today!). God, in His wisdom and power, turned this sad situation to the benefit of the church. Now there were two mission teams instead of one! Barnabas and Mark, and Paul and Silas set off in different directions to preach the gospel and encourage the believers. Barnabas and Mark went back to Cyprus (the home of Barnabas; where the first mission had begun) and Paul and Silas headed north, through Syria, back to Paul's home territory, Cilicia (verse 41). Paul (when known as Saul) seems to have been active in Tarsus when he was sent there for his own safety from Jerusalem (9:30). Churches were obviously planted by him throughout the region surrounding Tarsus.

Silas was an excellent choice of travelling companion and co-missionary with Paul. He was evidently highly respected by the Jerusalem church (verse 22) and would help give Paul added credibility in Jewish Christian circles. He was a Roman citizen, like Paul, (and unlike Barnabas) which would stand him in good stead for their dealings with the authorities (16:37). He was also a prophet (verse 32) and Paul seems primarily to have been a teacher (see comments on 13:1). This was precisely the 'ministry mix' which had worked so well for Barnabas and Paul on the first mission. It was a team which met with the approval of the Antioch church, who gladly and prayerfully sent them out (verse 40b).

Questions

1. *Should we only work in the church with people we like (verse 39)? How can we resolve personality conflicts? Are there ever 'irreconcilable differences' which would cause us to part company from our fellow workers?*

2. *Silas had lots of the right qualifications – both in ministry and background. What kind of 'qualifications' should we look for in a ... housegroup leader? steward? missionary? preacher/ teacher?*

3. *Why do you think 'teachers' and 'prophets' need each other? What happens in Church life when only one of these ministries is present?*

Acts 16:1–10

Timothy Joins the Team

Paul and Silas travel through Cilicia and arrive at the towns that were visited during the first mission. God actively helps plan the itinerary!

Back in Lystra (a town he is unlikely to forget in a hurry (14:8–20)), Paul discovers a believer called Timothy (verse 1). Timothy and his mother Eunice (2 Tim. 1:5) were probably converted in Paul's first visit to Lystra. Timothy was youthful (1 Tim. 4:12) yet had already gained an excellent reputation in the churches (verse 2) despite his
natural reticence (perhaps even shy? cf. 2 Tim. 1:7). He was educated by a Greek father but thoroughly versed in the Jewish Scriptures (2 Tim. 3:15) – no wonder Paul saw great potential in this young man.

Paul arranged to have Timothy circumcised (verse 3 need not mean he wielded the knife himself!). This should have happened in infancy, but perhaps pressure from a Greek father prevented it. Paul insists on this, as a special case, to put right an error (culturally) which had occurred. It has nothing to do with his Christian commitment; it simply recognises that Jewish boys are circumcised, so Timothy ought to be. Being a Christian did not mean a rejection of 'Jewishness' but a rejection of Jewish Law as the means of salvation! (cf. 4:12, 15:11).

So (after a few days to recover) Timothy and the missionary team leave Lystra (verse 4), taking the letter from Jerusalem and explaining its implications. These missionary visits result in local churches being built up spiritually and seeing growth numerically (verse 5).

The team were planning to push west into Asia, presumably to impact the major settlements of influence there (including, for example, the seven churches in Rev ch. 2 & 3). God told them not to do this, so they went north instead, hoping to minister up near the Black Sea (Bithynia). God again told them not to go, so they turned west, ending up in the Port of Troas, on the Aegean Sea (verses 6–8). Here Paul has a vision of a man pleading with him to make the 150 mile journey across the Aegean sea to Macedonia (verse 9). Paul responds to this 'at once' (verse 10) believing it to be a clear call by God to a new situation. (Notice 'they' becomes 'we' in verse 10 – Dr. Luke (Col. 4:14) seems to have joined the team, perhaps because Paul was sick?)

Notice that three times in this passage (verses 6,7,9) God supernaturally alters the destination of the travellers. This is His mission: the message is about Him, the Power is from Him and the directions are given by Him.

Questions

1. *How sensitive are we to God's guidance? Paul has a vision (verse 9). What methods does God use to guide? As a church? As individuals?*

2. *Timothy was young but widely appreciated (verse 2). What place do young people have in the ministry of your church? How can their gifts be discovered and released?*

3. *Timothy also knew the Old Testament well (see 2 Tim. 3:15). How can we increase our knowledge of the Bible? Why should we?*

Acts 16:11–15

Europe's First Convert

Paul, in obedience to God's call, travels to Macedonia. They find some women by the river in Philippi, and Lydia is converted – and offers the group hospitality.

With favourable travelling conditions, the mission-team sail from Troas to Neapolis (via the island port of Samothrace) in two days (verse 11). Neapolis is the port which served Philippi, and was only ten miles away. Philippi was a Roman colony (verse 12) which gave it considerable independence from the regional authorities and direct access to the emperor, and Paul undoubtedly saw it as a strategic place to establish a church. There does not seem to have been a synagogue, but the citizens of Philippi do appear to be aware of a small group meeting by the river (verse 13); Paul goes in search of it, and finds it just outside the city. They sit with the women and take the opportunity to talk with them about the gospel.

Lydia is there, a business woman who traded in up-market clothing ('purple cloth' verse 14); the congregation could well have been made up of business associates and members of her household staff. She already knows about God and Paul gives her the opportunity to know Him personally. This affluent woman, who is 400 miles from home, is moved by what she hears (verse 14b). She responds positively to the Good News. She and her household members are baptised (verse 15a) – perhaps there and then in the river (cf. 8:36, 9:18). The baptism is followed by an expression of practical hospitality. The mission-team would need somewhere to stay and she appears to have a substantial property. This generous offer would be very valuable to a group of travellers with limited financial resources. In any case, ancient hotels (inns) were expensive, dirty and not always safe. On the other hand, Paul and his team could not afford to be compromised in any way. They had to be sure that this was a bona-fide offer. Once they were sure, they gladly accepted (verse 15b).

This is hardly a momentous start to the mission in Philippi. The contrast with some other cities, where miracles and large numbers of converts are mentioned (e.g. 14:1,21), could hardly be more stark. The church in Philippi was started by three Jews (Paul, Silas and Timothy) and a Gentile (Luke) who had an initial congregation of one woman and her household! From this unimpressive beginning a sizable, generous, well organised church was established (See Phil. 1:1; 4:15,16).

Questions

1. Paul and his team go looking for people to share the gospel with (verse 13). How keen are we to seek out witnessing opportunities? What are the best places for you to tell others? (Church? Home? Shopping? School gate? Recreation Centre?)

2. Hospitality is important in church life. How many people have we had round for coffee/dinner recently? How can we develop the gift of hospitality (1 Pet. 4:9)?

3. From one convert, God built a church. How can we prevent ourselves from being discouraged when we only have a little (Little money? Few friends?) or if we are only a little church or small housegroup?

Acts 16:16–24

Thrown in Jail

The power of God confronts the Devil's power – and wins! An uproar sees Paul and Silas arrested, beaten and put in prison. Things look bad for the missionaries.

As they were going to the place of prayer by the river, the missionaries were intercepted by a girl possessed by an evil spirit (verse 16a). She has a demonically-inspired gift of foretelling the future and seems to have done so with some accuracy, judging by the large sums of money she was making for her 'employers' (verse 16b). She seems to have been drawn to the missionaries and kept yelling at the top of her voice about the fact that they were God's messengers telling about His plan of salvation (verse 17). (Notice a similar response to Jesus in Mark 1:24. The demon accurately identifies who He is.) This is free advertising for the missionary team, but not at a time or place, or in a manner which helps them. They certainly do not want to run the risk of being associated with anything occultic.

This shrieking goes on for days and days (verse 18a), and Paul can no longer bear to see this poor girl so dominated by the Evil one; nor does he want his lack of response to be misread as fear or powerlessness. Using the name of Jesus to full effect, he casts the evil spirit out. It leaves her, she is now silent and devoid of her ability to foretell the future (verse 18b).

Her bosses (with no apparent concern for the girl's personal well-being) are very angry at losing such a lucrative source of income. They drag Paul and Silas into the market square and demand punishment from the magistrates (verse 19). The scene in the market place is less than a riot but more than a 'scuffle' – enough for the magistrates to have a genuine fear that major public disorder could erupt. The girl's 'employers' incite the crowd by stirring up racial hatred and bigotry ('Jews' verse 20 versus 'Romans' verse 21) and by accusing them of encouraging Romans to break the law. The rule of law was of vital importance in the volatile cities on the edge of Europe. This accusation (and an angry mob!) panicked the magistrates into hasty, overly brutal action (verse 22).

The jailer is commanded to look after them carefully (verse 23) – the last thing the magistrates want is an escape and another near-riot on the streets. The jailer takes no chances: he puts them in the top-security cell and secures their feet (verse 24).

Questions

1. God defeats Satan (verse 18). What evidence is there of occult activity today? How can we help warn people of the dangers of ouija boards? Seances? Fortune-telling? etc.

2. Notice the concern about money (verses 16,19). Why is the love of money dangerous? What should our spending priorities be? How much should we give away?

3. Paul and Silas were beaten and imprisoned (verses 22,23), we are teased at work! Imagine how they would cope today. Imagine how you would cope then! What can we learn from this?

Acts 16:25–40

A Late Night Conversion

Paul and Silas sing and cause an earthquake! Their jailor becomes a Christian and they are set free. They leave the city.

Paul and Silas must have been in some pain after their brutal flogging, but they can still find enough energy to pray together and sing out loud – at midnight (verse 25)! Suddenly an earthquake shakes the prison and everyone's chains fall off (verse 26). The jailor knows that if a prisoner escapes he will have to take the punishment they would have had. Doubtless several of his prisoners were on 'death row', so he decides to kill himself to avoid torture and death at the hands of his superiors (verse 27). Paul assures him that no-one has escaped (verse 28). The jailor calls for some light to check this for himself and discovers that it is true (verse 29).

His response is amazing. He wants to know how to be 'saved' (verse 30). Had he heard Paul preaching in Philippi? Was he listening in on the prayers and songs earlier in the evening (verse 25)? All we know is that he has concern for his soul, and believes that Paul and Silas can help. Paul replies by pointing his captor to Jesus (verse 31 cf. 4:12, 8:12, 15:11). The jailor doesn't really understand the implications of this, so Paul and Silas take time to help him make an informed decision (verse 32). Baptism is the next step (verse 33 cf. Lydia, verse 15) followed by some basic medical attention and a little hospitality (verse 34a).

In the middle of all this suffering 'joy' is the overwhelming feature of this 'dead-of-the-night' scene (verse 34b cf. 13:52). In Acts suffering and joy are not opposites; in fact the former seems to stimulate the latter (5:41!)

At dawn, the magistrates send their assistants to order the release of Paul and Silas (verses 35,36), but Paul has other ideas. He is a Roman citizen and has rights which could not be easily trampled on. Silas shares this status, but they have both been flogged in public without a trial and imprisoned; all this is in violation of their rights as Roman citizens (verse 37a). Paul and Silas could have pressed charges but will settle for a little eating of 'humble-pie' (verse 37b). Luke records (with ill-concealed glee!) the worried magistrates scurrying to the prison to escort their 'guests' from the jail, no doubt with much apologising (verses 38,39). Lydia's house has become something of a base for the church (verse 40), so they return there to give a report on their exciting night and to encourage the brothers to stand firm (cf. Phil. 1:27,28).

Questions

1. *Do we only worship or pray when we feel like it (see verse 25)? Is our church attendance or private prayer-life affected by our feelings?*

2. *Lydia (verse 15) and the jailor (verse 33) were baptised immediately. Why do we tend to wait? Do you think there were any babies in the jailor's household? Were they baptised?*

3. *What does verse 31 mean? Write out an explanation in your own words. What would you have said in answer to the jailor's question?*

Acts 17:1-9

Preaching in Thessalonica

Paul and Silas preach and have a good response. Jealousy in some Jews provokes unrest, and Paul's host suffers. Another church is planted.

All of a sudden 'we' becomes 'they' (16:40b, verse 1a). Luke no longer appears to be with the group. He may well have remained in Philippi to strengthen the new church there.

The other members of the team travel south and then west, passing through two cities (without preaching?) and ending their 100 mile journey in Thessalonica (verse 1). This large city was a centre for trade and commerce, attracting a variety of nationalities, among them a sizable Jewish population. Paul, using the same method of operation which he had begun in Antioch (13:46, 'to the Jew first'), visits the synagogue. They appear to be open to discussion and debate, so Paul attends over a period of three weeks to present his case (verse 2). The preaching material is familiar: 'The Messiah is Jesus, and He died and rose from the dead. All of this was seen in the Old Testament Scriptures' (verse 3). Obviously Luke only gives us a summary of what Paul said; there would have been much quoting of scripture and some debate about what those Scriptures meant.

Despite the similarity of the material, there is a slightly different emphasis on the approach. There does not appear to have been a spectacular miracle to generate interest or faith. In Thessalonica, the thrust of the mission seems to be to convince 'intellectually'. Luke's use of 'reasoned' (verse 2), 'explaining' (verse 3), 'proving' (verse 3) and people being 'persuaded' (verse 4), all point to Paul's clear and thoughtful approach to his evangelistic task. Miracles were an important feature of the evangelism of the early church, but they were not the only feature! In the absence of a miracle, the gospel could still be communicated effectively and receive a warm response (verse 4).

As people begin to respond, jealousy again rears its ugly head (verse 5 cf. 13:45). Troublemakers, who are hanging around the shopping precinct, are recruited, and a mob begins a riot. They rush over to where the missionaries are staying so they can sort them out (verse 5)! Jason seems to have got wind of this and has hidden his guests. In the absence of Paul and Silas, Jason is the next best thing (verse 6). He is accused of harbouring criminals who are trying to overthrow Caesar and put a king called Jesus in his place (verse 7). The officials are anxious to avoid another riot but do not seem to have enough evidence for a conviction (verse 8). They are let out on bail (verse 9).

Questions

1. Is becoming a Christian a matter of 'faith' or 'understanding'? or both? Do you believe, then understand or understand and then believe?

2. Could you persuade (verse 4) people about your faith? How can we get good answers to some of the difficult questions? What questions are people asking?

3. The Christians were getting a reputation for being associated with riots (verse 5 cf. 16:20)! What has your church got a reputation for? – among other churches? In the community?

Acts 17:10–15

Preaching in Berea

Paul and Silas leave Thessalonica for Berea, where they find serious-minded people who study the Scriptures. Paul has to leave when trouble arrives but many are converted.

Paul and Silas had to leave Thessalonica in a hurry. It may well have been a condition of Jason's bail (verse 9) that he evicts his house guests, probably removing them from the city. The missionary team leave at night (in haste and secrecy) to travel southwest to Berea, fifty miles away (verse 10). Losing no time they head straight for their usual evangelistic starting point – the synagogue. Luke describes the Bereans in glowing terms, noting the stature of their characters and the serious, thoughtful way they respond to what Paul teaches (verse 11).

Luke contrasts the Bereans with the Thessalonians by applauding the way the former judge Paul's words on the basis of Scripture, not on considerations of culture, politics or even economics (cf. 16:19)! Many of the Jewish communities (not just in Thessalonica) seem to have little concern for 'truth'. The Christian message seems to be rejected not because it is untrue so much as because it is inconvenient! Some are jealous of the missionaries' success (verse 5), others are afraid that their status in the community will be affected or fearful of Roman reprisals. There seems to have been very little attempt to engage in serious debate about the issues.

The 'ignorant' Peter and John are flogged but not offered any serious response to their claims (4:13, 5:40). Stephen gives a massive, carefully argued speech and is offered no response but rage and stoning! And so it goes on. No wonder Paul is so delighted to come across a group for whom 'truth' is so important.

The people of Berea (Jews and Gentiles) come to faith in significant numbers (verse 12). Once news of this reaches Thessalonica, the Jews there sent their troublemakers to stir up trouble (verse 13). The situation was serious enough to remove the prime target (Paul) but safe enough for Silas and Timothy to remain behind to strengthen the new church (verse 14). They took Paul to the coast and then by boat to Athens – a sea journey of about 300 miles (verse 15).

At first sight, all the opposition which the missionaries experienced seems very discouraging; but it played a vital role in the spread of the gospel. The persecution forced them from town to town across Asia and Europe, taking the Good News as they went. God turned *their* problems into *His* opportunities!

Questions

1. How often do we dismiss things God says to us as 'inconvenient'? Or delay putting them into practice? Why do we ask ourselves how something will affect us before we ask whether it is 'right' (e.g. tithing)?

2. How can we learn to see our disappointments from God's point of view? Would you have thought all this opposition was good if you were Paul?! How can we allow God to take something bad that has happened, and use it for good?

3. What does it mean to be of 'noble character' (verse 11)? Which two words would you most like used about you? Why?

Acts 17:16–21

Opportunities in Athens

Paul sees Athens in all its cosmopolitan confusion and longs to change it. He preaches to Jews and Gentiles and provokes interest, but not immediate belief.

Athens had been the 'centre of the world' in the centuries before Paul arrived. Art, architecture, philosophy, cultural pursuits and decadence had all characterised this influential city. By the time Paul arrived it was a shadow of its former glory, with a population not in excess of fifteen thousand. But it retained the trappings of empire and was still a centre for the religious and philosophical viewpoints of the day. What distressed Paul so much was the idolatry everywhere (verse 16). He was wanting Silas and Timothy to join him, but he cannot hold back from presenting the gospel in this confused but significant city!

His two-pronged attack takes him to the synagogue (as usual) and to the commercial district where soap-box oratory is the order of the day (verse 17). He talks with anyone who will listen. Paul soon comes across the two leading ideas of the day. Epicureans thought gods were distant and uninterested in humans. Their goal was to achieve tranquillity by banishing fears, anxieties and particularly, concern about death. Stoics thought of God only in a vague sort of way, and emphasised the power of people to cope with their own lives and destiny, without divine intervention. Both groups had an 'absentee' god so Paul is immediately in conflict with them as he presents a personal God who sent a personal Saviour who could not be defeated by death (verse 18)!

Of course, some thought he was just a 'babbler' (verse 18a) and not worth listening to; while others thought that he was suggesting another god (whom they had not heard of) to add to their already extensive list! However, curiosity won the day and they brought him to the city Council (verse 19). The Council would have been responsible for issues related to religious freedom; and, given their reputations as intellectual men in the philosophical market-place of the world, they would have wanted Paul to have a fair hearing. Paul is asked to state the basic teaching he advocates, and to explain its implications (verse 20).

Luke does not seem to have much time for this sort of debate. As a practical man (a doctor, Col 4:14) he is dismissive of the Athenian theorists who can do nothing but talk, and listen to obscure facets of philosophy or some new debating point (verse 21).

Questions

1. *How many different religious viewpoints are there in your town? (List them.) Do any of them have any truth in them? How can we respond to this?*

2. *What kind of 'God' do we have? Does He get involved with our lives or let us get on with it? What did Paul think?*

3. *Are Christians in danger of being 'all talk' (see verse 21)? How can we make sure we are people of action, as well as talk? Why do we find talking easy and action hard?*

Acts 17:22–34

Paul's Athens Sermon

Paul addresses the Council of Athens and attempts to introduce them to Jesus. Some believe, but most remain unconvinced. A few are openly cynical.

This is a significant preaching opportunity for Paul, and he appears to have prepared carefully for it. The address is different in tone and content from his earlier sermons, which drew largely on the Old Testament for their material (cf. 13:16–41). (Paul is also at his most different here from the sermons of Peter cf. 4:8–12.)

Paul begins by affirming the Athenians. They would be glad to be thought of as 'very religious' (verse 22) – a tribute to their open-mindedness and intellectual tolerance. Paul had even discovered an altar to a god whose name they did not know (verse 23). This was either an altar put up to a god whose existence some had heard of but no-one knew much about, certainly not its name or specific powers; or an attempt to 'cover all the options', an altar just in case there turned out to be a god they had not heard of, who might not take kindly to being ignored! Paul seizes on this to provide an opening for his sermon – 'let me tell you who your unknown God is'.

The apostle cuts across all their understanding of little deities and points to God. 'This God made everything (verse 24) and certainly could not be contained in a human building (temple). He is utterly self-sufficient (verse 25) and in charge of the people in every country in the world (verse 26). He longs for men and women to find Him, and even though He is incredibly powerful and awesome, He is not difficult for humans to find (verse 27). Even your own poets (Epimenides and Aratus, are both quoted) point you in this direction (verse 28); and since we were created by God in His image, we must not think He looks like a statue of gold or silver (verse 29). The time for all that superstition is over. God calls everyone to turn back from this behaviour (verse 30) and get ready for the day of reckoning (verse 31) which is certainly coming! God has raised Jesus from the dead to prove this (verse 31b)'.

The last sentence blows them away – a physical resurrection they just can't swallow! Some jeer and mock, others defer judgement to another occasion (verse 32). A very small group respond to the message, and believe (verse 34). By his normal standards, the mission in Athens was a failure.

Questions

1. *Do you think people today are 'very religious' (verse 22)? What are their gods? How do they express their 'worship'?*

2. *Paul designed his sermon for this group specifically. What signs are there of this in the passage? How should all this affect our evangelism – as a church and as individuals?*

3. *Why do people find the resurrection of Jesus hard to accept (verse 32)? Should we tone it down to make it easier for them? Why is it important?*

Preaching in Acts

Acts records at least 14 sermons (or speeches) which explain the Christian message. They range from a 52 verse epic sermon (Stephen) to a one verse statement (Paul before Festus (25:8)). In each case we see how the material is tailored to fit the audience, without compromising its essential truth.

Paul's preaching in Athens is an excellent example of this. There are none of the usual references to the Old Testament Scriptures or Jewish history (which these Greek leaders would have little knowledge of); instead Paul uses a familiar visual aid (17:23) and quotes from two of their poets (17:28,29). Despite the clear difference of approach, the same simple response is called for (repentance 17:30) on the basis of the same truth (the resurrection of Jesus (17:31)) as in previous messages!

Paul's success as a preacher can be attributed (in part) to his ability to present the message in terms his hearers can relate to (cf. 1 Cor. 9:19-23), without diminishing its challenge or reducing its demands.

Acts 18:1–11

Paul in Corinth

Leaving Athens, Paul makes his way to Corinth for his next Mission. There are some significant people converted and Paul stays to teach and encourage.

Paul left Athens and made the ninety mile journey west to Corinth (verse 1). The two cities could hardly have been more different: Corinth was huge with perhaps as many as a quarter of a million inhabitants and was a centre for business, trade and commerce ... not idle philosophical speculation! The peoples of the world were represented in its population and within the city limits vice of every kind could be found.

Paul needed to provide his own board and lodgings, so went to work with a couple who had a tent-making business, Aquila and Priscilla (verse 2). They were travellers themselves, thrown out of Rome by the emperor (along with many other Jews) so would have been sympathetic to Paul's need for work. (They may have become Christians in Rome before coming to Corinth). They not only employed him, but found him accommodation with them (verse 3). This work still gave Paul time for regular Saturday trips to the synagogue to present his message (verse 4 cf. 17:2).

Silas and Timothy eventually catch up with him (probably bringing money from the Philippians (Phil. 4:14f)) and this frees Paul to go back into 'full-time' preaching (verse 5). The message of Jesus the Messiah produces its usual hostility from the Jews (verse 6 cf. 14:2, 17:5) and in an Old Testament-style prophetic gesture (verse 6b) he turns away from them to minister to the Gentiles (cf. 13:46). Paul moves his headquarters next door to the synagogue (a bold, if undiplomatic, move!) and continues preaching. Amazingly, the most senior figure in the synagogue is converted and – no doubt helped by the example of Crispus – many other Corinthians believe and are baptised (verse 8).

Paul must have arrived in Corinth in a pretty discouraged state. Athens had been a failure and he may not have felt fully recovered from the beating in Philippi (16:23). Persecution in most of the towns he visited meant that he had to move on, but God had something different in store here. God gives Paul a vision which assures him of divine support and encourages him to be bold and fearless (verse 10). This 'word' came at just the right time to prevent discouragement from spoiling his ministry. Armed with this message he stays in Corinth for eighteen months; evangelising, and also discipling new converts (verse 11).

Questions

1. *Do you think clever, intellectual people are harder to reach with the gospel than others? What are their difficulties? How can they be overcome?*

2. *Is 'full-time' Christian work (verse 5) the ideal for everyone? Why do we need full-time 'tent-makers'? Is for example accountancy less of a calling than a Bible college tutor?*

3. *Should Christians ever get discouraged? What can they do about it? How can we help each other?*

Acts 18:12–17

Paul and Gallio

The Jews make a determined effort to undermine Paul and his ministry. The Proconsul throws their case out of court, as a matter of purely Jewish concern.

Gallio probably became Proconsul about half way through Paul's stay in Corinth, and the Jews thought this new ruler may be sympathetic to their cause. They brought Paul to the sizable platform or stage area, which was elevated in the market place in Corinth. Here the Proconsul would hold court, giving his verdict on various cases (verse 12). They tried to claim that Paul was advocating a religious view which had not been declared legal by Rome; and so he was breaking the law (verse 13). This was a serious charge, and if believed, would have severely curtailed the opportunity for Christians to preach across the Roman empire.

Paul is about to launch into his defence when Gallio (known in the ancient world for his fairness, charm and wit!) responds for him (verse 14). Gallio refuses to accept the charge against Paul, believing it to be a minor squabble between various factions of Judaism. He sends them away to sort out their own problems amongst themselves (verse 15). There is more than a hint in this passage that he believes they are wasting the court's time. They, and their case, are thrown out of court. Even when they turn savagely on their own leader (perhaps Sosthenes became ruler when Crispus became a Christian (verse 8)) he refuses to be drawn into the debate (verse 17). The matter is closed!

Luke portrays a rational and fair Roman legal system which would not allow itself to be embroiled in religious issues unnecessarily; nor be manipulated (by the beating of Sosthenes) into an 'anything-to-keep-the-peace' response. Gallio himself emerges from this episode with great credit. The Jews of Corinth do not. Their accusation is unfair and their methods dubious. God had promised Paul that no harm would come to him (verse 9) and this decision is seen as part of the fulfilment of that vision. On a larger scale, this Proconsul has done the Christians a huge favour by not 'finding for the Jews'. Other Roman authorities would take note of this decision and take their 'cue' from it. Christianity had not been banned and Gallio had demonstrated his displeasure at being bothered by such a matter. Jews in other areas would think carefully before calling in the Roman authorities in their dispute with the Christians!

Questions

1. Do you think it would make a big difference if Christianity was banned? Where would we meet? How would we evangelise? Would we be stronger or weaker than we are now?

2. God kept His promise to Paul (verse 9). Why do we find it so hard to trust God? Do you think Paul ever doubted?

3. Paul was not breaking the law (verse 13) but Christians in some countries have to if they are to be faithful to God! Is this right or should they obey the law anyway (see 5:29)? When are we not bound by the law of the land?

Acts 18:18–28

Starting the Third Mission

**Paul returns to Antioch, via Ephesus, and prepares for another mission-
ary journey. Apollos is also used powerfully by God among the Jews.**

Because of Gallio's decision, Paul is free to remain
unhindered in Corinth (verse 18). But he seems to have
taken a vow of some kind (a Nazarite vow? cf. Num.
6:1–21) which involved shaving his head and he may
have wanted to return to Jerusalem to offer thanksgiving
to God. Paul may have made this vow to be faithful, in
response to God's promise (verse 9) and was now wanting to offer some
kind of thanksgiving in Jerusalem. He was thoroughly converted to
Christianity, but was a *Jewish* Christian, whose culture still mattered a
great deal to him.

He took Aquila and Priscilla with him (perhaps they paid for the trip!)
and they boarded a boat at the port which served Corinth, Cenchrea, and
sailed east to Ephesus (verse 19). Paul visited the synagogue but could
only stay briefly (verse 20). He left Aquila and Priscilla in Ephesus and set
off by sea to Caesarea (verse 22) – a journey of over six hundred miles!
From Caesarea he 'went up' (almost certainly this means to Jerusalem) and
met with the church; after seeing the Jerusalem Christians (and giving an
offering for the fulfilment of his vow?) he went back to Antioch.

After what may have been about a year in Antioch, he sets off on his
third missionary journey (verse 23a); retracing his steps of the second
journey, visiting the churches and encouraging them in their faith.

Luke interrupts his account of Paul at this point by introducing us to

Apollos. Apollos is a Jew from the Egyptian city of Alexandria. He was an educated man who was thoroughly familiar with Old Testament Scripture (verse 24). He had obviously come across the teaching of Jesus and had responded to it as best he could. He certainly knew who Jesus was (verse 25) but seems not to have fully grasped all the implications of the information he had heard. Fortunately, Aquila and Priscilla were on hand to fill in the gaps in his education and experience (verse 26). After a period of discipleship, he felt drawn to Achaia, and ultimately found his way to Corinth (verse 27 cf. 1 Cor. 3:6). The Ephesian Christians encouraged him in this venture and he proved to be an invaluable asset to the Christians there. A brilliant orator and skilled debater, he took the Jews on, on their own territory – the Old Testament Scriptures. He showed conclusively that Jesus was God's chosen Messiah (verse 28)!

Questions

1. Notice Paul's commitment to 'God's will' (verse 21). How aware are we of God's purposes? How can we be more sensitive to God? How can we 'discover' His will?

2. It's easy to have 'incomplete knowledge' (verse 25). How can we make sure we grow in our knowledge? How can we encourage others to grow in their knowledge?

3. Apollos was corrected in private (verse 26). What does this teach us about correction and confrontation? Why is such correction necessary?

Acts 19:1–10

Paul in Ephesus

Paul arrives in Ephesus and discovers some disciples of John the Baptist. He explains the gospel to them and they believe. Others are more resistant – but the gospel spreads.

Paul has travelled from Antioch north and west to Galatia and Phrygia (18:23), then pushed due west to the Aegean sea port of Ephesus (verse 1). He had been well received when he was last here about a year ago (18:20) and approached the city with a degree of expectation. His first task is to sort out some confusion – a dozen men (verse 7) seem to have heard about Jesus, even claiming the title 'disciple', but their faith seems defective. And this is a defectiveness of a totally different order from the experience of Apollos (cf. 18:25, 26). Not only have they not received the Spirit, they had never heard of the Spirit (verse 2)! They have simply expressed repentance as taught by John the Baptist (verse 3 cf. Mark 1:4).

Paul preaches to them about the one John pointed to (cf. John 1:29,30) as God's Messiah – Jesus (verse 4). Once they understood that Jesus, not John, was the focus of attention, they wished to be baptised in His name (verse 5). As Paul prayed for them they were filled with the Holy Spirit, and burst out in tongues and prophetic words (verse 6). This experience is similar to the one enjoyed on the first Pentecost (2:4), in Samaria (8:17) and at Caesarea (10:46). The order of events may vary – repentance, faith, water-baptism, Spirit-filling – and the 'signs' of life may vary, but all these components seem to be required for full Christian initiation.

We notice that Apollos was defective in understanding but these 'disciples' were defective in fact and focus. Apollos needed to see Jesus more clearly, these men needed to see Him for the first time! We also note from this passage how clearly the Holy Spirit came. As in other places in Acts, the Spirit's coming was not without its 'signs' (e.g. 4:31, 8:18). We must be careful not to reduce His coming to a form of words or a mere ritual, however orthodox and correct the form of words may be. Form is never an adequate substitute for reality!

Paul makes regular visits to the synagogue over a period of twelve or thirteen Sabbaths, trying to persuade the Jews about Jesus and His kingdom (verse 8). Some refuse to believe and begin to make life difficult for Paul and the Christians (verse 9) so he rents a hall from Tyrannus, a local lecturer with a fearsome reputation among his students (Tyrannus = tyrant!). For two years this ministry continues (verse 10) and the Good News continues to spread.

Questions

1. Is the Holy Spirit real to us or a phrase we know? How can we move from knowing about God to knowing Him? Should we expect any 'sign' of His power in our lives?

2. Even after all this time (and negative response!) Paul has not given up on the Jews (verse 8). What does this teach us about patience? Why do we give up so easily? How can we develop tenacity?

3. How do you feel when you are criticised (see verse 9)? What is the natural response? What is the right response? Should you over defend yourself?

Acts 19:11–22

Miracle v Superstition

The last months of Paul's ministry in Ephesus are characterised by many great miracles and the exposing of satanic forces. Honour comes to the name of Jesus.

Even by Paul's usual standards (which are pretty spectacular!) this period of ministry has an amazingly large number of miraculous events (verse 11). The workman's aprons he used in tent making and the cloths he wipes his sweat off with, in the heat of the day, are all used to bring healing and release from demonic powers (verse 12). In Ephesus this sort of thing would not be unusual, but in Paul's case, the healing was not due to 'magic cloths' or 'lucky aprons'. The healing power lay in God Himself, and the faith in Jesus of the sick person receiving the cloth or apron.

Some local Jewish exorcists thought they would add a new technique to their deliverance repertoire, using the name of Jesus (verse 13). It backfired horribly on them when an evil spirit spotted the deception and said, 'Jesus and Paul I know, but who on earth are you?' (verse 15). They received a terrible beating at the hands of the demonised man (verse 16) ... and presumably did not try it again.

News of this incident spread like wildfire and the name of Jesus became highly honoured. People were afraid of this name (Jesus) and those who wielded its power (the Christians). (This is not unlike the response to the death of Ananias and Sapphira (5:11).) It brought people out of the woodwork who had not confessed their occult involvement (verse 18).

They may have kept some of the literature secretly at home but now it all comes out into the open. They want to make a totally fresh start. Everything they have which has been used in an occultic way, anything which is part of their superstitious past ... is burnt publicly (verse 19). A huge sum of money goes up in flames! No wonder the gospel grew after such public testimony to its power (verse 20).

After this, Paul decided that he ought to return to Jerusalem (verse 21) – perhaps to give a full report to the church leaders there. His long-term plan was to revisit the churches he had planted, report back to Jerusalem, then head off to Rome. He was not quite finished in Ephesus, so he sent Timothy and Erastus on ahead (verse 22). They could begin the task of encouraging the churches and let them know he was coming.

Questions

1. Many Ephesians burnt their parchments (verse 19). How should we separate ourselves from the wrong things in our past? (e.g. should we throw away 'questionable' books?) Can our past have a hold on us? How should we act when we think it does?

2. Why is occult involvement wrong? What does it result in? How can freedom be obtained?

3. Do you take the name of Jesus seriously enough (see verse 17)? Why is a casual attitude dangerous? What difference would it make to our worship if we understood the true power and honour of Jesus' name?

Acts 19:23–31

Jesus v False Gods

As Paul prepares to leave Ephesus, those who profit from the worship of Artemis stir up a riot. Some of Paul's friends are caught up in the disturbance, but Paul remains free.

Such is the success of Christian activity in Ephesus that the established religion comes under threat. Ephesus had long been a centre for the worship of Artemis – a many-breasted goddess of nature and fertility. With the increasing demise of Ephesus as a commercial centre, it had to look to pilgrims and tourists for a larger amount of its income. Anything which threatened this would have been viewed extremely seriously. Followers of 'the Way' (verse 23 cf. verse 9) were doing precisely this!

Demetrius, a man whose living was made casting figurines of the goddess in silver, was afraid that his livelihood was being threatened. He called together his fellow workers (and others in allied trades) to discuss ways of responding to the crisis (verses 24,25). These men are losing money, and if things continue as they are, they stand to lose a good deal more. In a desperate statement he pays (unwitting) tribute to Paul's success as a missionary and the growth of the church (verse 26). The result of Paul telling people about Jesus is that they see the statues which Demetrius makes as irrelevant at best and evil at worst – certainly not as gods! Two things followed from this: 1) 'we are going to be out of a job' and 2) 'the great goddess will not be worshipped as she ought to be' (verse 27).

It seems fairly obvious that we are not dealing here with some pious, religious men, who have a disinterested commitment to the honour of their goddess! They are motivated by their pockets (not altogether surprisingly) but their devotion to Artemis is the pretext on which they hope to build their case against the Christians. In the ancient world, it seems it was more acceptable to put a man out of work than to discredit his god!

The crowd of tradesmen soon motivate an angry mob, all shrieking, 'great is Artemis of the Ephesians' (verse 28). Gathering momentum, they force two of Paul's travelling companions to join them (verse 29) as they charge eastwards across the town to a large open-air theatre; the city assembly met here. They want to force an emergency session of the city council. Paul is keen to address the crowd (never one to miss an opportunity!) but the Christians are opposed to this (verse 30) and even some of the civic leaders who are sympathetic to Paul's position, warn him against appearing before the crowd (verse 31).

Questions

1. *If the vast majority of people became Christians tomorrow, what occupations would be unnecessary? What jobs make less money if you have to be completely honest? How can we support Christians in difficult work situations?*

2. *Paul had some wise friends (verses 30,31). Do we care enough about anybody to try to stop them doing something we think is wrong? Do we have friends like this? Where can we get them from?*

3. *Artemis was a false god. What are the 'false gods' in society today? How do they influence our friends and neighbours? (and us?!)*

Acts 19:32–41

Peace is Restored

The shouting mob continue to yell their support of Artemis. Not until a senior member of the Council appears is there some quiet. Reason prevails and order is restored.

In the large theatre where the crowd had assembled, things were going from bad to worse. People were shouting out different things and most of them did not know what was really going on (verse 32). All the majority knew was that in some way Artemis was being threatened; beyond that there was ignorance and confusion.

The Jews had certain privileges in Ephesus and would have been keen to distance themselves from the Christians, in case they were accused along with them. Alexander was appointed spokesman and tried to speak to the crowd (verse 33). Once they realised that he was a Jew they drowned him out with their chanting (verse 34). To most Ephesians the subtle difference between Jews and Christians would count for little in this intense environment. They both had no time for idols. They were the cause of the problem, not its solution.

After two hours of this, the senior non-Roman leader in Ephesus appears – the city clerk. He reminds them that the position of Artemis in Ephesus is known everywhere, it needs no defending. Given this fact, they ought not to jeopardise their standing in the world by this rash act (verses 35,36). The tourist trade is far more likely to be damaged by rumours of civil unrest than it is by the Christians. The crowd should remember that. What's more, Gaius and Aristarchus have committed no crime; they are not guilty of robbery or blasphemy against Artemis (verse 37). If anyone wants to press charges, let them do it through the law courts (verse 38), and other matters can be brought to the regular civic assembly (verse 39, it may have met as often as three times a month). Then the city clerk raises the 'Roman' dimension. The Romans were generally quite lenient on their conquered nations, but civic unrest was an unacceptable expression of public feeling. It was sometimes crushed by the Romans with terrifying ferocity. The city clerk was wanting the crowd to be clear about the possible consequences of their actions, and to dissuade them from any similiar action in the future (verse 40).

There was no justifiable reason for the unrest, they should go home (verse 41). The city clerk comes across as a brave, wise man. He refuses to be panicked or manipulated into persecuting the Christians (see comments on Gallio (18:12–17)).

Questions

1. *When have we seen mob action in modern society? What are the results? How should a Christian march or gathering be different?*

2. *The clerk is full of wise advice (verses 35–40). Where do you go to in a panic, for 'wise advice'? What kind of counsel should local churches provide? Why is common sense so uncommon?*

3. *Alexander was shouted down (verse 34). How do we respond to people we disagree with? How can we learn from these disagreements? How should we treat these people?*

Acts 20:1–12

Travelling and Encouraging

Paul leaves Ephesus to visit his churches in Macedonia. In Troas, a long sermon and a miracle strengthen the believers.

Paul had already decided to leave Ephesus (19:21) and the riot must have confirmed that this was the right course of action. He gathered the believers together to say goodbye and to encourage them to stand firm in the Faith (verse 1), then he left for Macedonia. He travelled, preached and encouraged his churches on the journey
west to Greece (verse 2). Luke sees these return visits to churches as 'encouragement'. Of course, a certain amount of correction, even rebuke, would have been necessary; but it is all couched in the most positive of terms. Paul's ministry is as an 'encourager' (verses 1,2 cf. 14:22, 15:32, 16:40).

After three months in Greece he travelled back through Macedonia on land, to avoid being drowned at sea in a Jewish plot (verse 3). Paul's travelling companions went on ahead to Troas, but he sailed from Philippi after the Feast of the Unleavened Bread – a trip which took over twice as long as a previous crossing (verse 6 cf. 16:11,12). Paul was collecting money for the needy church in Jerusalem (cf. 1 Cor. 16:1–4) and the men with him were representatives from the donating churches. They would accompany him to Jerusalem to present the gift on behalf of their fellow-believers. A large sum of money was being accumulated, and there would be a little more security in a larger group travelling together (verse 4).

169

Luke has rejoined the missionary team (probably in Philippi verses 5,6) and the descriptions of events involve his eye-witness observations. 'On the first day of the week' (verse 7) they gather to celebrate the Lord's supper. This is the first clear indication of the growing emphasis on Sunday (the resurrection day!) in the Christian community. The movement away from the Sabbath to Sunday would increase rapidly as the first century moved on.

The evening meeting went on for some time, and the combination of a long sermon, lack of oxygen and fatigue caused Eutychus to fall asleep. He was sitting on a window ledge and fell to his death, while asleep (verses 7–9). Paul and the others went down the three storeys to see if he was alright (he wasn't!) and an incredible miracle occurred – he was brought back to life (verse 10). After a 'midnight feast', Paul talked until dawn and then left (verse 11). What an amazing night it had been! Paul's superb instruction and teaching, a communion service, fellowship over a meal and somebody raised from the dead – no wonder they went home 'greatly comforted' (verse 12).

Questions

1. *Why did the Sabbath change to Sunday? How is it different? How should we celebrate Sunday? How can we help those who have to work on Sunday?*

2. *How can we develop 'encouragers' in the church (see verses 1,2)? Why do we have so many 'discouragers'? How can we give some practical encouragement to our leaders?*

3. *Death is defeated (verse 10) but Eutychus would die again in the future. Why is death such an avoided subject? If Jesus has defeated death, in what ways can every Christian experience an even greater miracle than Eutychus?*

Acts 20:13–27

The Journey Continues

Paul is anxious to get to Jerusalem for Pentecost and travels by boat and land to get there. He says goodbye to the Ephesian elders.

The group of missionaries and church representatives set sail for Assos (verse 13) but Paul decided to walk. (Perhaps to teach a little longer in Troas and enjoy some time alone with God as he walked on the coastal road from Troas to Assos). They all met up in Assos and went south, visiting various ports until they arrived at Miletus (verses 14,15). Paul chose to miss Ephesus, probably because the riot would still be in his mind (19:23f) and because he wanted the minimum delay on his journey to Jerusalem (verse 16).

Miletus was thirty miles south of Ephesus and Paul asked the Ephesian leaders to meet him there (verse 17). He seems to be filled with sadness at the thought of not seeing them again (verse 25) and may well have had fears for the future. He uses this occasion to review the past, describe the present and prepare them for the future. It is a sermon filled with personal passion, practical teaching and theological reflection; almost a mini-epistle!

Despite trials and opposition, Paul has humbly tried to preach the gospel in Asia. He has spoken to individuals and to crowds, Jews and Gentiles – all with the same message: turn around from wrong and believe in Jesus (verses 18–21). Now he feels called to go back to Jerusalem, though having no idea what to expect (verse 22). God has warned him not to expect an easy life (verse 23) so he goes to Jerusalem with his eyes wide open. But however difficult it may get, in Jerusalem or anywhere else, Paul's priority is clear. His life means nothing in itself, he has only one aim: to tell people about the wonderful grace of God (verse 24). This 'grace' is understood by Paul, both personally and theologically. He can never get over the fact that an unworthy persecutor of the church like him (9:1–19 cf. 1 Tim. 1:12–16) should be forgiven and entrusted with this missionary task. Nor is he unaware of God's purpose for humanity as a whole; undeserving though we are His Son has died for us, and risen again! (see 2 Tim. 1:9–11).

Paul has done his duty, he has faithfully proclaimed the gospel. No one will be able to blame him for not speaking out what he knew of God's plan and purpose (verses 26,27).

Questions

1. Paul knew what his 'calling' was (verse 24) and fulfilled it. How can we know what our calling is? Who could help us find out? What should we do about it?

2. Paul is very aware of God's grace (verse 24). What has God saved you from? What might you have become? Why is it important to be reminded of this?

3. Paul has proclaimed the whole will of God (verse 27). Why do we have a tendency to emphasise only bits of it? Why is this dangerous? How can we be more 'complete' in our emphases?

Acts 20:28–38

Encouraging the Elders

Paul concludes his address to the Ephesian elders with words of challenge and encouragement. He leaves for Jerusalem amid scenes of painful farewells.

Paul encourages these church leaders to take good care of their own spiritual lives and those of the people of God, given them to care for (verse 28). Just as Jesus was the Good Shepherd (John 10:11), they are to be under-shepherds for the sheep Jesus gave His life for. As shepherds they must be alert for all the enemies of the sheep (verse 29) – people from outside the church (and, sadly, some from within it) will attempt to spoil what God has begun in Ephesus (verse 30). They are to be alert boxers, never letting their guard down. Paul has given three years of his life in preparing them for this moment (verse 31).

Paul sees the role of overseer as a protector against false teaching. Even the pastoral image of shepherd is used in the context of protection against wolves. Many Christians today see leaders as being available to meet *their* needs and solve *their* problems. Paul sees them protecting from attack, so the ministry of evangelism can continue. Shepherds are to feed, lead and protect the sheep ... not to carry them!

The apostle then commits these leaders to God's grace – He is the only one who can strengthen them and keep their future secure (verse 32). Then he adds a note about becoming greedy for money (verse 33). Covetousness is a terribly destructive thing, especially in a leader. Paul had worked as a tent-maker (cf. 18:3) so no one could accuse him of 'free-loading' on the church (verse 34). Another antidote for greed is to make sure that they are generous to the poor and those who cannot care for themselves. This is just what Jesus would have wanted them to do. (In verse 35 Paul quotes a saying of Jesus not recorded in the Gospels. Perhaps he heard it from one of the 'twelve', when he was in Jerusalem.)

When he has finished, Paul kneels in prayer with them all; brothers together in Christ (verse 36). Many tears were shed on this sad day (verse 37); they were losing a mentor, a brother and a friend. The parting was especially painful because they thought they would never see him again (verse 38). Right until the last moment they could, they wanted to be with Paul, so they went down to the dock-side with him.

Questions

1. What do you want from your leaders (see verse 28)? Is it the right thing? Do congregations demand too much?

2. Is money a problem in our churches (see verses 33–35)? Why are we so materialistic? Are we generous to the poor? Are we paying our leaders properly?

3. Some teachers distort the truth (verse 30). How can we know what is sound teaching? Who should we trust? How can we avoid becoming suspicious of everyone?!

Acts 21:1–9

The Journey to Caesarea

Paul leaves the Ephesian elders at Miletus and travels south and then east to Caesarea. A safe journey ends in Philip's house, with his family.

Leaving the Ephesian elders is a huge emotional wrench (verse 1) and the journey to Cos cannot have been tear-free! The ship travels south from Cos to the island of Rhodes, and then on to Patara. Here they find a ship going across the Mediterranean, and board it immediately (verse 2). Their route takes them east from Patara, out into the Mediterranean, passing within sight of Cyprus and then on into Tyre; this 450 mile journey probably took about five days (verse 3).

The ship then spent a week at Tyre, unloading its cargo and taking on supplies. Paul used this opportunity to meet with local Christians. Some of them, with prophetic insight, saw what dangers lay ahead in Jerusalem. This was not news to Paul (cf. 20:23), although the prophecy may have been more specific than he had previously been aware (verse 4). The prophecy obviously had a profound effect on the church in Tyre; all of them, including the women and children, went with Paul back to the boat. The prayer time on the beach had similarities with his farewell to the elders at Ephesus (verses 5,6 cf. 20:36). He hardly knew these believers but the ties between Christians (especially in a hostile environment) can be very strong, even when there has been no time for a relationship to develop in the normal way.

The voyage continued 25 miles south to Ptolemais where a brief meeting occurred with local Christians (verse 7) and then on another thirty miles, down to Caesarea. Here the travelling missionary team end their travel by boat. They find accommodation with Philip the deacon-evangelist (6:5, 8:4f). Philip seems to have moved his centre of operation from Jerusalem to Caesarea (verse 8). He may have been based here for as long as twenty years. Luke specifically mentions his four daughters, who had a prophetic ministry (verse 9). As the ties to the male-dominated Judaism weaken, a meaningful role for women becomes more and more possible. They may have chosen to remain unmarried to fulfil this prophetic calling more completely; or it may simply have been the lack of suitable believing young men in the Caesarean church. (A situation not without its similarities to today!) Philip's daughters would have played a part, no doubt, in his evangelistic missions and the life of the local assembly.

Questions

1. Why do Christians form such strong ties with each other? What binds us together? Is there ever a final goodbye from one Christian to another?

2. Philip's four daughters obviously had a valuable ministry (verse 9). Do women play a significant role in church life today? How can they be encouraged? Why should they be?

3. Paul travelled thousands of miles for the gospel's sake. Why does the church today find it so hard to send people overseas for the sake of the gospel? What holds us back, as individuals, from going? How can we change this?

Acts 21:10–16

Journey to Jerusalem

Paul is on the very last stage of his journey to Jerusalem. Despite a warning of trouble, he travels to his destination to celebrate the feast.

Paul, probably weary from his travels and busy schedule, takes a week or two to rest at Philip's house (verse 10). He wants to arrive in Jerusalem refreshed and no doubt uses the time at Caesarea to prepare himself emotionally and spiritually as well. After a few days Agabus arrives. He has a well-known and tested prophetic ministry (cf. 11:28). On this occasion he illustrates his prophetic words with a dramatic visual aid. Using Paul's belt, he ties his own hands and feet, indicating that the owner of the belt will be bound like this in Jerusalem (verse 11). The Jews will hand Paul over to the Gentile authorities.

Just as in Tyre (verse 4), the disciples in Caesarea and the rest of the travelling missionaries, urged Paul not to go on to Jerusalem (verse 12). They are good friends to Paul with his best interests at heart; they plead (with tears) that he should not place his life in jeopardy. But Paul is absolutely determined to go. He is ready not only to be arrested, but if necessary, also to die (verse 13).

Paul was keen to celebrate Pentecost in Jerusalem – a significant Jewish feast with very powerful Christian memories (cf. 2:1f). He may have been driven by the desire to take the money he had collected and deliver it personally to the church in Jerusalem, but there is a greater underlying determination here. He is motivated by the Spirit (20:22) and operating under a divine compulsion. Nothing will distract him from this goal. (It is all reminiscent of the experience of Jesus. He knew what awaited him in Jerusalem and yet was determined to go there (Luke 9:51).

When they can all see that Paul's mind is made up, they stop pleading with him and commit him into the Lord's hand (verse 14). This is not a resigned fatalism but a positive affirmation of what they see as God's will in this situation: humanly speaking he should not go to Jerusalem, but the Lord wills that he should (cf. Jesus in Matt. 26:39b).

Together they travel the 65 miles to Jerusalem (verse 15) where they are given hospitality by Mnason, one of the earliest converts (verse 16). The third missionary journey has been completed and Paul is back where he feels compelled to be.

Questions

1. Paul was determined (verse 14) to go to Jerusalem. Where did this determination come from? Why is determination important? How can we develop it?

2. What is the difference between determination and stubbornness? How can we tell the difference? Do we really listen to those who advise us?

3. 'The Holy Spirit says' (verse 11). List the ways in which God speaks to us today. How can we recognise His voice? What role do church leaders have in this?

Acts 21:17–26

With the Jerusalem Leaders

Paul tells the Jerusalem church about his missionary journey. He corrects a misunderstanding by helping some Jewish Christians, and undergoes purification himself.

As on Paul's last visit to Jerusalem (15:4), he was warmly welcomed by the local Christians (verse 17). After this initial welcome (perhaps at Mnason's house) a meeting was arranged for the following day. James, the leading figure in the Jerusalem church, along with all the elders, gathered to hear a detailed report of Paul's ministry among the Gentiles (verses 18,19). They were thrilled to hear of all the miraculous events, conversions and churches being planted; but they did have a problem (verse 20).

Thousands of Jews had been converted in Jerusalem and surrounding areas – most of them keen to retain their Jewishness. Some of them had heard a rumour that Paul was encouraging Jews to turn their backs on their heritage (verses 20,21). Gossip and rumour were rife in the ancient world (have things changed?!) and it is not difficult to see how this sort of impression could be created by reports of Paul's ministry in Asia and Europe. (Despite the fact, for example, that he had had Timothy circumcised 16:3.)

The Jewish leaders suggested that Paul 'sponsor' four poor Christian Jews who wished to undertake a Nazarite vow (as he had done some years earlier, 18:18). This will involve him in certain purification rites himself, but also be seen as a pro-Jewish act of kindness (verses 23,24). This will demonstrate that Paul continues to see himself as a Jew *and* a Christian; he will show that he is committed to the gospel, but not therefore opposed to Jewish culture and tradition. Paul, wishing to correct the misunderstanding, is happy to comply with their request. The Jewish Christian leaders, for their part, are anxious to confirm that the agreed requirement for Gentiles (verse 25 cf. 15:29) still stands – they are not bound by Jewish law.

The very next day (Paul loses no time as this is only his third day in Jerusalem) he goes to the temple with the four men and begins the task of purifying himself and them. He then informs the temple authorities of the date the purification will end and that he will provide an offering for them at that time (verse 26). Paul is very keen to send out the right signals to the Jewish Christians. He would never compromise on the issue of obedience to the law (cf. Gal. 2:11f) but he did not wish to deny his Jewishness, nor cause unnecessary offence to his fellow Jewish believers.

Questions

1. *Do you have to be part of English-speaking middle-class culture to be a Christian? In what ways do we force people to accept our culture with our Christ, when they come to church? How has this tension been seen in our missionary work?*

2. *Is there any gossip in your church (see verse 21)? How can we correct rumours? How can you prevent yourself contributing to the gossip 'circle'?*

3. *Paul and God had worked together among the Gentiles (verse 19)! How much is God's responsibility and how much is ours, in Christian work? Is it an equal partnership? Could God do it without us?*

Acts 21:27–36

Paul is Arrested

On a visit to the temple Paul is attacked by Jews, falsely accused and nearly beaten to death. He is 'rescued' by a Roman commander, and arrested.

When he is almost at the end of his period of purification, Paul is spotted in the temple by some Jews from Asia; perhaps Ephesus. They recognise him as the cause of much tension in Asia and seize the opportunity to stir up the crowd against him (verse 27). Religious zeal is at fever pitch and the temple would be packed with pilgrims because of the Feast of Pentecost. They accuse Paul of speaking against two of the pillars of Judaism – the Law and the Temple. To this half-truth they add a straightforward lie for good measure. They say that Paul has brought Trophimus (the representative of the church at Ephesus, 20:4) beyond the court of the Gentiles into the inner court, where only Jews were allowed (verse 28).

Luke explains that the only ground for saying this is that they had seen Paul and Trophimus together in the city earlier (verse 29). Paul knew that the punishment for this was death, and he is hardly likely to encourage persecution when he can get plenty of it without trying! However, such is the religious hysteria, that minor considerations (like the truth!) are swept away in the mob violence which follows. Paul is dragged to the outer courts, the inner gates are closed to prevent defilement from any bloodshed, and the crowd begin to beat Paul to death (verses 30,31).

Once news of the riot reached the Roman authorities the commander mobilised his soldiers. He dispatched some officers and their men from the fortress of Antonia (to the north of the temple) to pull Paul out of the crowd (verse 32). He is promptly arrested and dragged off back to the fortress for interrogation. Try as he might, the commander could not get any sense out of the crowd. People were shouting conflicting things and this, combined with the sheer volume of noise and the continuing violence, made it impossible to get at the truth (verses 33,34).

The commander is determined to find out the facts and has Paul half-dragged, half-carried away from the temple and back to the relative calm of the fortress (verse 35). The crowd followed them, screaming out 'away with him' (verse 36). Judging by what they meant when they said the same thing about Jesus (Luke 23:18) this amounts to a demand for Paul's execution!

Questions

1. *Which religion/philosophy is the most negative towards Christianity today? Which group in your community is most negative toward the church? Why? What can be done about it?*

2. *Why do people believe lies so easily (verse 28)? Why is telling the truth so important? Is exaggeration a lie? Or not saying anything?*

3. *Religious fanaticism (verses 30,31) continues today. Why do so many bad things happen in the name of religion? Why is religious hatred often so intense? What causes this 'blind' devotion?*

Acts 21:37–22:5

Paul Addresses the Crowd

As he is being taken away, Paul asks to speak to the crowd. His defence begins with his credentials as a Jew and his persecution of the Christians.

As Paul is being pulled up the steps into the fortress he asks the commander a question in Greek. The commander would have been surprised to be addressed in the usual language of the Roman Empire, by someone he thought was an ignorant rabble-rouser from Egypt (verse 38). Three years earlier an Egyptian had gathered 4,000 men on the Mount of Olives, hoping for an opportunity to overthrow Roman rule in Palestine. They were defeated by the Roman army, but it was a serious enough uprising for the commander to remember it ... and not want it repeated (verse 38).

Paul tells the commander that he is a Jew from a significant and influential city, Tarsus (verse 39). He then asks if he may speak to the crowd. This request is granted because the commander hoped to discover what the problem was between Paul and the crowd; he may also have been more kindly disposed towards Paul because of his Greek language skills, and his general manner in such trying circumstances. Paul asks for silence and begins to speak in Aramaic, the local language. This surprises the crowd and wins him a marginally more sympathetic hearing (verse 2).

The speech in his own defence begins (as Stephen's speech did, 7:2) with a respectful, and yet warm, greeting (verse 1). It is delivered to an almost exclusively Jewish audience. Paul explains that he was born a Jew and had a Jewish upbringing; that he had studied with the almost legendary Gamaliel (cf. 5:34) and had completed his training in Jewish law. He was extremely 'zealous' in his Jewish faith (verse 3). Not only that, he put his commitment into action against the followers of 'the Way' (verse 4 cf. 9:2, 19:9). Neither men nor women had any mercy from him, so zealous was he to uphold the Law.

And all these facts can be born out by the Council, who both authorised and approved these actions. Paul even cites the High Priest as someone who could testify to the truth of what he is saying (verse 5a)! He had even pursued the Christians beyond Jerusalem, obtaining special permission to hunt them down in Damascus (verse 5b).

This is an impressive set of credentials. The crowd would be totally in agreement so far ... but the speech isn't over yet!

Questions

1. Could you describe your 'Christian' commitment in such glowing terms (see verses 2–5)? What do you think is involved in being a 'zealous' Christian? Would your church leaders describe you as 'a keen, committed church member'?

2. The commander made a mistaken judgement (verse 38). Why are we so quick to judge by appearances? Are we overly impressed by someone's accent? Clothes? Job? Why do these things affect us?

3. Paul's upbringing was important to him (verse 3). What does this imply for Christian parents? Children's work in church? Child evangelism?

Acts 22:6–21

Paul's Defence Continues

Paul moves from his Jewish background to the story of his Christian conversion. The speech ends as he is describing his call to preach to the Gentiles.

After establishing his thoroughly Jewish background (verses 3–5) Paul proceeds to describe his encounter on the Damascus road (verses 6–17 cf. 9:3–19). This account is very close to the original story earlier in Acts, but with the distinctly Jewish elements highlighted. Paul is accurately describing what happened to him, but placing the emphasis on certain things in order to communicate most effectively to this specific audience. (e.g. Ananias is described as being a 'devout observer of the law and highly respected by all the Jews' (verse 12); and, 'The God of our fathers' and 'the Righteous One' (verse 14) are distinctly Jewish phrases.)

So Paul describes what happened to him on the journey from Jerusalem to Damascus. He is blinded (verse 6), confronted (verse 7), chosen (verse 14), called (verse 15) and baptised (verse 16)! This dramatic story would have had the crowd reeling, as each new development was unfolded before them. It is a story of miraculous events, supernatural voices and stunning words. The account of a life turned upside down. Paul is at his passionate best as he recalls that amazing day, all those years ago.

On his return to Jerusalem he describes a visit to the temple (notice the continuing 'Jewish' emphasis) where he had a supernatural visit from Jesus (verse 17) telling him to leave Jerusalem quickly because his message would provoke unrest (verse 18 cf. 9:29,30). Paul was acutely aware of his reputation as a persecutor of Christians (verses 19, 20) and believes it will be difficult to find acceptance among them. After all (and here Paul re-emphasises the strength of his earlier Jewish convictions cf. verses 4,5) he has hunted the Christians down, had them imprisoned and beaten; and was even party to the murder of deacon Stephen.

Despite all this, Paul is accepted by God (and the Christian community, cf. 9:26,27) and commissioned to take the message 'far away to the Gentiles' (verse 21 cf. 9:15). The Gentiles were 'far away' in two senses: Paul would have to travel many miles from Jerusalem to fulfil this commission, and the Gentiles were not 'near' to an understanding of God and His ways, as the Jews were (cf. 2:39).

Paul never got complacent about the sinfulness of his past, and was forever grateful for the grace of God in forgiving, and then commissioning him to such a great task!

Questions

1. Do you have a dramatic conversion story? Do you need one? Which facts are more important than 'when' you were converted?

2. Paul's testimony is clear (verses 6–16). Can you describe what happened to you? Write it down. Put it in the church magazine or ask to tell your story to the house group.

3. Do you have a difficult past (verses 19,20)? How can you be free from it? Is anything too bad for God to forgive? Can we start again?

Acts 22:22–30

Paul the Roman Citizen

The crowd interrupt Paul and demand his death. To prevent a flogging he claims that he is a Roman citizen. A hearing is arranged.

The crowd had listened with approval to Paul's account of his Jewish background (verses 3–5) and with interest to his amazing conversion story (verses 6–16), but his remarks about being called to the Gentiles (verse 21) make their blood boil. To claim that Jews and Gentiles could have access to God on an equal basis was more than they could stomach. They break into his speech, demanding his death (again! cf. 21:36), claiming he is not fit to live (verse 22). They make their point in a typically eastern manner (verse 23) stripping off for action and throwing dust and dirt into the air – and the commander obviously fears a riot of major proportions. Paul is whisked inside the fortress and prepared for questioning (verse 24).

The commander could not understand what the crowd were yelling, nor could he have understood Paul's defence in Aramaic. He is beginning to lose patience with the whole business. He orders Paul to be brutally flogged, in order to extract a confession. (This is quite different from the beating he received, for example, at Philippi (16:23). The scourge was an instrument of torture, which could cripple for life or even kill. It is not the simple whip or rod of Paul's earlier experiences!) The time for gentle enquiry is over!

Just before this potentially life-threatening beating takes place, Paul announces that he is a Roman citizen (verse 25). This sends the centurion scurrying to the commander and the commander back to Paul (verse 26) to confirm the truth of his claim (verse 28). Roman citizenship was an honour shared by a privileged group; even a Roman commander had no automatic right to it. This commander had paid a huge sum of money to obtain this privilege; but Paul is able to boast that he was born into the privileged position (verse 28). This puts an entirely different complexion on things. The torturers quickly disappear and the commander is relieved that he found out in time. To put a Roman citizen in chains was bad enough (verse 29) but to have had him flogged would have been a very serious offence indeed.

Paul was kept in custody overnight (presumably for his own safety) and brought to appear before the Jewish council (verse 30). No doubt the commander believed that it was primarily a religious question, so he ordered the highest authority on religious matters to meet, and give Paul a hearing.

Questions

1. Paul was a Roman citizen (verse 25). Does your citizenship give you any advantages when presenting the gospel? How has your country helped your life as a Christian? How has it hindered?

2. Torture is still used to extract confessions (see verse 24). What can we do about this? How can we support Christians who are abused in this way? Why is it so easy to be complacent?

3. The Commander had a difficult job. Was he justified in resorting to violence against Paul? What aspects of your job do you find difficult? Do you ever feel forced to compromise your faith? Could you be a Roman officer and a Christian, for example (cf. Cornelius, 10:1)?

Acts 23:1–10

Paul Before the Sanhedrin

Paul is brought before the Sanhedrin and cleverly divides them into two factions. They can't agree on a verdict. Paul returns to the fortress.

Paul begins his statement to the Council with a description of his conscience – it is clear (verse 1 cf. 20:26). Paul simply means this to be taken at face value, he has not wilfully done anything he knew to be wrong. The high priest believes it to be an arrogant claim and instructs Paul to be hit in the face (verse 2) by those nearest to him. The action is in direct violation of Jewish legal procedure (where a man was innocent until proved guilty) and makes Paul very angry. He calls the action hypocritical and he insults the high priest with a familiar term of abuse (verse 3) – 'You are a poor excuse for a wall. A rotten, broken down pile of bricks disguised to look like a decent wall with a thin coat of paint!' (Paul spoke more accurately than he knew. Ananias was a corrupt and greedy collaborator with the Romans. He stole from the priests, gave bribes and was open to them. He eventually died at the hands of his own people. God did judge him! verse 3a).

The Council is amazed at Paul's language to the high priest (verse 4) – they are all terrified by the wealthy and influential Ananias. Paul apologises immediately (verse 5 quoting Exodus 22:28) wanting to honour the office of high priest, if not Ananias the man. As Paul is regaining his composure he remembers the natural divisions which exist on the Council and decides to exploit them (verse 6). He may well have given up any hope of a fair hearing after the action of Ananias; and anyway the Sanhedrin did not exactly have a good track record when it came to dealing with Christians (4:5f, 5:40, 7:54f). He may well be trying to avoid similar treatment to that received by the early apostles, rather than giving a reasoned defence.

He claims to be on trial for his beliefs as a Pharisee (particularly the resurrection of the dead) and this sets the Council in uproar. The Sadducees are against him and the Pharisees for him. 'Who are we to judge this man if God has spoken to him', the Pharisees argued (verse 9). All the old prejudices rise to the surface and the Sanhedrin is split on party lines, with more than verbal abuse being thrown! The commander fears for Paul's safety and breaks up the meeting by force, taking Paul to the safety of the fortress (verse 10).

Questions

1. Did Paul lose his temper (verse 3)? Was he wrong to do so? Should we ever lose our temper? What should we do when it happens (see verse 5)?

2. Did Paul tell the truth when he divided the Council (verse 6) or was it just a clever trick? Is it ever right to lie? In what circumstances? Should Paul be praised or condemned for this tactic?

3. Paul had a clear conscience (verse 1). Do we? How can we get a clear conscience ... and keep it that way? Why is this important?

Acts 23:11-22

Escape from Conspiracy

Paul is assured by Jesus that he is going to Rome. A plot to kill Paul is discovered and the Roman Commander is alerted to the danger.

Paul, now back in his cell, may have been feeling fairly despondent after the troubles of the last few days. At this moment, his Lord appears to him with a message of reassurance and hope (verse 11). His longing to preach in the empire's capital (cf. 19:21) would be fulfilled! Paul must have rested more easily, and with a lighter spirit, after this Divine encouragement.

He may not have been quite so relaxed had he known what was being planned by forty fanatical Jews who had taken an oath to neither eat nor drink until Paul was dead (verses 12,13)! It confirms our fears about the corruption in high places, when we learn that this gang has no qualms about telling the chief priests about their plot (verse 14) and even asking for their help (verse 15). Ananias and his cronies have no scruples when it comes to protecting their own interests. But Paul's nephew finds out about the plot and visits Paul to tell him (verse 16). (Paul is under the equivalent of 'house arrest'. He is not free to leave but he could have visitors and would have been reasonably well cared for.) Paul asks that his nephew be granted an interview with the commander (verse 17) and a confidential discussion takes place (verses 18,19).

Somehow Paul's nephew has acquired detailed information about the plot. Was his father invited to join the forty men? Local gossip? Is he a servant to the Jewish 'elder' (verse 14)? And he describes it all to the commander (verses 20,21), who takes it very seriously. Even though he is only a boy (early teens?) his story has the ring of truth and there seems no obvious reason for making it up. Besides the commander is aware of the current Jewish mood and the character of Ananias. This plot is not unlikely.

The experienced Roman commander wishes this private conversation to remain confidential, so he cautions the teenager to tell no-one about the visit (verse 22).

Jesus has promised Paul that he is going to Rome (verse 11) and this incident shows Him fulfilling His word. A human agent discovers the plot, but we can hardly fail to see a divine hand behind it. It takes nearly three years for Paul to get to Rome – through many crises – but God is faithful to His word.

Questions

1. *God encouraged Paul (verse 11). How does He encourage us today? What should we do when despondency strikes? Look out for people who seem 'down'. What can we say or do to help them?*

2. *Paul's nephew took a big risk in going to the fortress (verse 16). Would you have gone or 'kept your head down'? Do we do the right thing even if we risk losing – a job? a friendship? money? prestige?*

3. *Here is a brave, responsible teenager! (see verse 17 'young man'). Was he a 'typical' first century teenager? Why are modern teenagers so heavily criticised? What is your church doing to help them? How are their gifts being used?*

Acts 23:23–35

Paul at Caesarea

The plot is thwarted by sending Paul to the Governor, Felix, in Caesarea. The carefully guarded Apostle arrives with a covering letter. He awaits trial.

The commander loses no time in responding to the warning from Paul's nephew (verses 20,21). That very day he arranges an escort to take Paul to the Governor in Caesarea. The size of the escort underlines the gravity of the situation as far as Claudius Lysias (the commander) is concerned. Two hundred infantry, seventy cavalry and
two hundred light-infantry ('spearmen') – nearly five hundred soldiers in all (verse 23)! – take Paul by night to Antipatris, a town thirty five miles away in the Judean hills (verse 31). Paul is provided with a horse to ride and a horse or mule for his belongings (verse 24). The foot soldiers return to Jerusalem the next day and the cavalry escort Paul the final thirty miles into Caesarea (verse 32).

The covering letter (verses 27–30) explains to Felix the situation and the need for the heavily armed escort. The gist of the letter accurately conveys what has happened and why Lysias is sending Paul to Felix. However, it is hard not to find aspects of the letter amusing; it seems unlikely that Paul would have felt 'rescued' (verse 27) by a Roman commander who did not actually find out about Paul's citizenship until much later in the day (verse 27 cf. 21:33 and 22:26). The absence of any mention of Paul in chains or the narrowly-avoided flogging of a Roman citizen indicate a certain selective memory loss, on the part of the Jerusalem commander! The whole process seems to be a buck-passing exercise. Claudius Lysias cannot discover the root of the problem and certainly does not want a Roman citizen assassinated while in his custody. 'Let's get governor Felix to sort it out'.

This self-congratulatory letter was handed to Felix by a cavalry officer (verse 33) and Paul was transferred into the custody of the governor of Judea. Felix asks Paul where he is from (if he was from another Governor's district or subject to another local authority Felix may wish to refer him to them, cf. Pontius Pilate with Jesus in a similar situation, Luke 23:6,7). When he discovers that Paul is from a Roman province (Cilicia) he feels able to deal with the situation himself (verse 34). When his accusers arrive from Jerusalem, Paul's case can be heard. In the meantime, a cell in what was Herod's palace will be his home (verse 35). Paul would be safe and not uncomfortable, being treated with a measure of care and respect.

Questions

1. *Is the letter from Lysias (verses 27–30) entirely truthful? Is it legitimate to paint ourselves in a good light? (On an application form? In an interview?) At what point does this become dishonest?*

2. *Was Lysias evading his responsibility by sending Paul to Felix (verse 24)? In what ways do Christians 'pass the buck' instead of accepting responsibility? (e.g. 'it's the leaders' fault'?) Why do Christians find it so hard to say – 'it was my fault'!?*

3. *The last time Paul was in Caesarea it was in happier circumstances (21:8). How do you think Paul coped with all the ups and downs in his life? Does your commitment to God (and the church) change depending on the circumstances?*

Acts 24:1–9

Paul's Trial Begins

After a brief wait in Caesarea, Paul and his accusers are brought face to face. The trial begins with the Counsel for the prosecution bringing his case.

As soon as he possibly can, Ananias arrives in Caesarea to finish the job he wanted done in Jerusalem. The Council had failed to make the 'right' decision (cf. 23:9) and the plot to kill Paul had been thwarted (23:23). Ananias is hoping this will be third time lucky, and he has come to court in person, hoping to guarantee the outcome. He has with him some of his colleagues from the Jewish eldership and a skilled legal expert called Tertullus (verse 1). Ananias must have been pretty confident in his team, particularly given the reputation of Felix as a greedy, praise-hungry man, not averse to being bribed (see verse 26). Here was a kindred spirit for Ananias – a man he could do business with!

Paul is called into the courtroom, and Tertullus is given permission to present the case for the prosecution. What follows is a fawning hymn of praise to Felix; even by the standards of the ancient world, where flattering rulers was the usual practice, this is 'over-the-top' crawling (verses 2,3). Felix was a cruel butcher who had put down Jewish uprisings with brutal ferocity. Hardly a single Jew would have agreed with Tertullus' description of Judea under Felix and even less would have had 'profound gratitude'! Tertullus moves on from appealing to Felix's vanity to present the charges against Paul.

There seem to be three specific charges:

1. He causes riots among Jews wherever he goes
2. He is ringleader of a troublesome sect
3. He tried to bring a Gentile into the forbidden part of the temple (verses 5,6).

The basic thrust of the charges is that the 'Roman Peace' is being threatened by Paul, who is a political agitator. Felix has crucified those guilty of this in the past and Tertullus is hoping for a similar verdict. Felix will find all this is true when he interviews Paul for himself, Tertullus concludes.

This is a remarkably brief speech (even briefer than Tertullus promised, verse 4) so presumably Luke has only given us an outline of the main points. However long the speech actually was, the Jews certainly liked it. They added their own murmurings of approval and agreement (verse 9). These Jews may have come from Jerusalem with the main accusers (verse 1) or they might be Caesarean Jews who had been 'encouraged' (bribed!) to be present in court, to support the charges.

Questions

1. Is flattery a sin (see verses 2,3)? In what situations are we tempted to do it? What does it say about us? What does it say about the person we flatter?

2. Paul must have felt outnumbered and 'outgunned'. Are there any situations when we feel overwhelmed by the opposition? How do we cope if we are isolated and alone? What makes us feel like giving up?

3. How do you feel when you are falsely accused (verses 5,6)? Should you defend yourself or be silent? How can you avoid self-pity or moping? How can you cope with the desire to 'get even'?

Acts 24:10–21

Paul Defends Himself

Paul is given the opportunity to present his defence to the court. He dismisses the charges against him and gives his side of the story.

Rather than cross-examine Paul, Felix gives the apostle the opportunity to make a speech in his own defence. Paul begins by affirming the value of Felix's long association with the region (about ten years) and how glad he is to speak in front of someone who was not a stranger to Jewish practices and belief (verse 10). This is a polite, positive and honest opening to his speech which must have contrasted sharply in the eyes of the court with the flowery, insincere praise of Tertullus (cf. verses 2,3).

Paul quickly dismisses the three charges against him. It is less than a fortnight since all this happened and he had only just arrived in Jerusalem. Hardly enough time to organise a revolt of some kind. He was not the 'ringleader' of anything. He was worshipping alone in the temple, peacefully and without any attempt to incite anyone (verses 11,12). As for the charge about desecrating the temple, it simply is not true, so they obviously cannot prove what they are saying (verse 13)! Paul admits his background as a Pharisee, and draws the Court's attention to areas of agreement between himself and his accusers. He does not deny that he is a follower of 'The Way' (verses 14,15). Believing in a resurrection, he tries to live his life with a clear conscience, knowing that one day he will face God (verse 16 cf. 23:1).

The point of Paul's defence is to describe the issues in religious, rather

197

than political terms. He is not dangerous to the Roman empire, seeking to overthrow any institution by force or intrigue. He is in conflict with his fellow Jews about matters of religious faith and practice; and even in the conflict, there are some areas of common understanding.

Paul goes on to spell out in detail why he had come to Jerusalem. His purpose was two-fold: to bring money he had been collecting in Asia and Europe for the poor and to bring offerings for himself to worship at the Feast of Pentecost (verse 17). He repeats his innocence of the charges by asserting that his religious preparation was complete and that his worship was not causing any commotion (verse 18). Religious and political offence was avoided by his behaviour. His real accusers are absent from the trial (the Asian Jews who stirred up the trouble in the first place, verse 19 cf. 21:27), no doubt because they had nothing that would stand up in court! The Sanhedrin could not find him guilty of a crime (verse 20) and neither will the Court of Felix – unless believing in the resurrection is a crime (verse 21).

Questions

1. *Verses 10–21 is the third opportunity Paul has had to 'present his defence' since arriving in Jerusalem. Could you 'defend' why you are a Christian? What would you say in your 'defence'?*

2. *They called Christians a 'sect' (verse 14). What is a 'sect'? Who are the sects today? What kind of things do they believe?*

3. *Verse 17 shows worship and care for the poor as priorities. Is one without the other unbalanced? Why do we need both? Which of the two do you think your church should emphasise more? (Both?!)*

Acts 24:22–27

A Long Adjournment

Felix closes the trial without a verdict. He hears Paul privately, but won't decide for or against him. Paul spends two years in custody.

Because of the link Felix has had with Judea over a number of years (see verse 10) he has come across followers of 'The Way' before and at least has passing knowledge of some of the issues involved (verse 22). He fobs off Ananias and his team with a lame excuse about waiting for the Roman commander to come and give evidence (verse 23) but he already has a written statement from Lysias! (cf. 23:26–30). The fact is, he knows Paul is innocent but does not want to offend the Jews. He is stalling for time. At least Paul is looked after well during his period of detention (verse 23).

Drusilla was Felix's third wife. He had lured her away from her husband (a Syrian king) with promises of wealth and power. He was attracted by her youthful beauty. The relationship was built on his lust and her greed. Perhaps because of Drusilla's Jewish background they arranged to hear Paul for themselves, privately (verse 24). Paul spoke freely about Jesus and about faith in Him. No doubt this involved his personal testimony and the presentation of supporting evidence from the Old Testament Scriptures. However, Paul was keen to press home the lifestyle implications of the Christian faith. The three areas he touched on must have made them squirm: neither had behaved with 'righteousness'. 'Self-control' was not exactly his strong point ... so no wonder they feared 'the judgement to come' (verse 25)! This was not the sort of talk they were expecting and they found it all a bit frightening. Paul is quickly dismissed and, as far as we know, Drusilla never hears him again. Felix will hear Paul again when he has had a chance to push some of the more challenging aspects of his teaching to the back of his mind!

Felix is caught between his fear and his greed. He finds what Paul says unsettling but he hopes for a sizable bribe to set him free (verse 26). Perhaps he thought Paul had wealthy connections or that his friends might raise the money. Certainly the thought that Paul would consider a bribe morally wrong, would not have occurred to this covetous, manipulative governor!

Felix eventually goes too far in brutal excess, when he viciously stamps out a problem between Jews and Greeks in Caesarea – largely by killing lots of Jews. He is recalled to Rome. For two years Paul has been waiting for a verdict (verse 27) – perhaps the new governor will give one.

Questions

1. *Christian faith has moral implications (verse 25). How does our faith affect our view of money? Sex? Possessions? Is it possible to 'believe' but ignore the moral implications?*

2. *What do you think Paul did for two years (verse 27)? Was it 'wasted' time? How can we avoid wasting time?*

3. *'Bribes' are still common in some parts of the world (see verse 26). How would you react if you had to bribe an attendant for a place to park your car or to get a parcel from home out of storage? Would you pay? Is bribery wrong in a country where there are low wages?*

Acts 25:1–11

Festus and Paul

The new governor arrives and is made aware of Paul's situation. A new trial is arranged and the same issues arise. Paul appeals directly to Caesar.

After taking only three days to settle in (verse 1), Festus makes his way to Jerusalem to meet the Jewish leaders. Felix has left a legacy of distrust and disharmony in Judea, and Festus is keen to make a start in restoring goodwill. (Festus seems to have been an excellent governor. Much better than Felix, or those who followed him in the office of governor. Sadly, he died after only two years in office.) No sooner has he met the senior Jewish leaders than they outline the case against Paul (verse 2). Hoping to take advantage of the new governor's innocence, they ask for Paul to be brought back to Jerusalem – hoping to have him assassinated en route (verse 3, they had tried this same technique over two years earlier – 23:12f!). Festus thwarts this plan (probably quite by accident) by insisting that the trial is held in Caesarea. Paul is already there, Festus must have been anxious to get his governorship established in Caesarea and the leaders can travel back with Festus and his advisors (verses 4,5).

After a little more than a week, the group make their way down to the coast to the Roman capital of Judea; the court is convened and Paul is brought in (verse 6). The Jews repeat the same old charges and Luke reminds us that although these charges are serious they have no proof (verse 7). They did not have any proof in the trial before Felix (24:13) and the last two years have not produced any either. Paul replies that he is innocent – he is not in breach of Jewish Law, did not desecrate the temple and has not broken Roman Law (verse 8). Stalemate! We are back to square one. Festus can see no way of resolving this, so he asks if Paul will go to Jerusalem to face the charges (verse 9). Paul is much more aware of the Jewish tactics than Festus, and knows his life would be in danger. What is more his experience over the last few years causes him to have more faith in Roman justice than Jewish injustice – where he is now ('Caesar's court') is where he wants to be tried (verse 10 cf. 18:12–16). Both Paul and Festus know that Paul is innocent of the charges (verse 10b) but they also both know it would be political 'suicide' to free someone so hated by the Jewish establishment. Paul bails them both out of a tricky situation by appealing to Caesar (verse 11).

Questions

1. *Festus is an improvement on Felix. What do you think made him a better governor? What characteristics should we see in our political leaders? What standards should they live by?*

2. *God ensures Paul's safety. What evidence is there that God has over-ruled in your life? Looking back, can you think of cases where God was at work and you were not aware of it? Can God use non-Christians to get His will done?*

3. *Paul stands up for his rights (verse 11). Would it not have been more 'Christian' to agree to Festus' request? When is it wrong to 'turn the other cheek'? What kinds of issues should we stand up and fight for?*

Acts 25:12–22

Agrippa and Paul

Festus agrees to send Paul to Rome. King Agrippa is visiting Festus and they discuss Paul's case. Agrippa asks to hear Paul first-hand.

Festus meets with his advisors to discuss Paul's appeal to Caesar (verse 12). As a Roman citizen, Paul had a right of appeal direct to the emperor. This right could be exercised if a Roman citizen was on a charge for which the death penalty might be appropriate. The charge of political revolt which the Jews claimed about Paul, could be punishable by death in a Roman court so his appeal to Caesar would have to be allowed.

When a neighbouring king came with his sister to greet the new governor (verse 13), Festus thought it would be good to enlist his help with Paul. (What on earth would he write in his report to the emperor?) Agrippa was known as an expert in Jewish matters, so Festus picks his brains about the problem which Felix had left him to resolve (verse 14).

Festus gives a fair summary of the situation, confessing freely his confusion (verse 20) and his surprise at the nature of the charges (verse 18). They appear to him to be totally concerned with religious matters and he cannot see any reason why Paul has to be tried by a Roman court. He offered Paul the chance to appear before the Sanhedrin in Jerusalem (verse 20b) and he declined, choosing rather to take his case to Rome. Festus informs Agrippa that Paul will be held in Caesarea until arrangements can be made to send him to Rome (verse 21). This could take months to plan – Festus would have to write a report, documentation for travel be prepared, a route to Rome worked out, financial arrangements made, etc. It was a journey of about 1,800 miles. No small trip in the ancient world!

Agrippa is fascinated by this case and asks to meet Paul and hear his side of the story. Festus promises to make this happen on the following day (verse 22).

Festus' report to Agrippa contains a vitally important phrase which sums up the nub of the issue perfectly – it is '... about a dead man named Jesus whom Paul claimed was alive' (verse 19). The resurrection of Jesus was at the heart of apostolic preaching (cf. 2:31, 3:15, 4:10, 5:30, 10:40, 13:37, etc); and was not simply an abstract theory – the first apostles had seen Him (2:32) and so had Paul (1 Cor. 15:8) – but a living personal experience. Jesus is alive!

Questions

1. Festus admits to not knowing what to do (verse 20). How ready are we to admit our weaknesses? Why do we pretend not to have problems? How can we recognise pride in our lives?

2. Festus consults Agrippa (verse 14). Who do we share our decisions with? Are we good at taking advice? Where can we get wise counsel from?

3. Jesus is alive (verse 19)! How do you know this is true? What evidence is there? Why is it important that Jesus did not stay dead? Do you think Christians have got blasé about this truth?

Acts 25:23-27

Festus and Agrippa

Festus calls together the 'leading lights' of Caesarea to join Agrippa in listening to Paul. He needs advice on what to say to the Emperor in his report.

Paul could not have arranged a better evangelistic opportunity if he had tried! Festus arranged for all the local dignitaries and the senior military personnel in the area to join him for a glittering social occasion. They process in, wearing their fine robes and dress uniforms amid much pomp and ceremony (verse 23). Agrippa and Bernice are
the guests of honour and once they have been seated, Paul is brought to stand before the group.

Festus gets proceedings underway by explaining why he has called everyone together. It all revolves around Paul (verse 24a). (Paul must have looked out of place in the opulent arena. He probably felt fairly isolated – a Daniel in a den of Romans – yet he controls all the proceedings by his presence. In God's eyes, everyone else was out of place; Paul was in the centre of His will.) The Jews have petitioned Festus (both here in the capital and in the holy city of Jerusalem) to have Paul executed (verse 24). Festus does not believe that the charges hold water; but anyway, Paul has appealed to the Emperor (verse 25) so Festus has no choice but to send him to Rome.

But what can he say to the Emperor about the case? He may not have wanted to admit that he was appeasing the Jewish leaders, so could not let Paul go. A charge of religious controversy (within Judaism) would be dismissed by the Imperial Court as outside its brief and a charge of political sedition was unproved. Festus knew this, (25:10 cf. verse 25). What was he to say? With this dilemma in mind he has called the group together to discover a way forward (verse 26). He can hardly send a prisoner all the way to Rome without some kind of letter of explanation (verse 27).

This is a remarkably frank speech from a new governor – very open and honest. He is not afraid to ask for their help nor confess his own weakness. Through it all Luke sees the hand of God moving clearly and certainly toward the fulfilment of his promise to Paul (23:11).

Through all the human confusion God is working His purpose out. Festus thinks he is the one sending Paul to Rome (verse 25), but a larger plan than the Governor of Judea knows about is being put into operation!

Questions

1. *Do you feel 'out of place' sometimes as a Christian? At work? At home? How can you deal with this feeling? How does God feel about it?*

2. *Who is in charge in the world (see verse 25)? Who is going to decide when the world should end? Is God more powerful than your boss at work? ... or the President of America?*

3. *Festus wants to please the Jews or he would release Paul (see verse 9). Is it possible to want to please people too much? Or please the wrong people? Or please people more than please God? What dangers are there here?*

Acts 26:1–11

Paul Begins his Presentation

Paul gets an opportunity for a full presentation of his position. He starts with a little background to the trial and a statement about his orthodox Jewish past.

Festus hands chairmanship of the occasion over to Agrippa, who invites Paul to speak. With an orator's gesture of respect for the chairman, Paul begins (verse 1). It was the custom to begin such occasions with words of affirmation (cf. 24:2,3) and Paul offers his sincere appreciation for Agrippa's grasp on Jewish issues. He is pleased to be able to address such a distinguished group and delighted that its chairman has such a long family association with the Jews. He asks for patience, so he can deliver an extended explanation (verses 2,3).

Paul was brought up as a Jew in Tarsus and Jerusalem, all the Jews can testify to this (verse 4). He became a Pharisee and was known for his strict adherence to the letter of the Law (verse 5). All Pharisees live in the expectation of the resurrection which was promised us by God, generations ago (verse 6). The whole nation is desperate to see it, so why should it be so amazing if God raises the dead (verses 7,8)? Paul simply believes what many of his colleagues in Judaism share – a belief in the resurrection.

And yet Paul is sympathetic to those who find it impossible to believe that Jesus is the one in whom the resurrection power was demonstrated. Indeed, as a good Pharisee, he became convinced that he should do everything in his power to oppose the growing influence of this man from Nazareth (verse 9). And he was not happy for his opposition to be merely theoretical; he arrested and imprisoned the followers of this Nazarene and even voted for their death (verse 10). He had visited many synagogues, in Judea and further afield, in order to stamp out the influence of the Christians (verse 11).

Paul is trying to show that his Jewish heritage is certain and that his Jewish credentials (as a Pharisee) are impeccable. Not only that but his belief in the resurrection (the central issue at stake here, cf. 25:19 and 23:6) is entirely orthodox. Jews ought to have no problems in the *possibility* of someone being raised from the dead. He then goes on to affirm how difficult it must be to accept the resurrection of Jesus – a fact he fought against 'tooth and nail' in the beginning. He really does understand their problem!

Questions

1. *Agrippa understood Judaism (verse 3). How well do we understand the 'Jewish' background to our Christian faith? How can we get to understand it better? Why is it important?*

2. *Paul understood those who disagreed with him. How well do we understand our non-Christian culture? What is the real reason your neighbours do not go to church? What do they really think about the Christian faith?*

3. *Paul had been where his accusers are (verses 9–11). Have we taken time to 'walk in their shoes'? Do we really know what it is like to be ... hungry? Bereaved? Lonely? 5,000 miles from home? How can we begin to understand these situations?*

Acts 26:12–23

Paul's Testimony

Paul describes the incident on the Damascus Road – his encounter with Jesus. He then tells how he has tried to put into practice what he was told.

Paul continues with his theme of persecuting the Christians (verse 12 cf. Gal. 1:13). He uses this as a 'bridge' into his conversion story; the third time Luke has recorded it for us (verses 12–18 cf. 9:1–18, 22:4–16). As usual, the basic facts are reported, with additional elements in order to communicate most effectively to this particular audience.

Paul emphasises the dramatic nature of the experience: light 'brighter than the sun' (verse 13), 'we all fell to the ground' (verse 14) and the short saying about kicking 'against the goads' (verse 14) highlights the internal struggle Paul was having. What a battle it was for this Pharisee to turn and follow Jesus!

Paul is wanting to emphasise the divine element in his call so Ananias does not get a mention. Paul is not being dishonest, simply recounting God's words without identifying the human agent who delivered them. He wants to demonstrate to this illustrious gathering that it was God *Himself* who convinced him and turned his life around. This same God commissioned Paul to tell Jews and Gentiles about Him: darkness would be turned to light, the devil defeated and God put in His place in people's lives, wrong things would be forgiven and the status of being one of God's children granted to those who believed (verses 17,18).

After this amazing encounter, Paul only did what anyone would have done in these circumstances – obeyed the voice from heaven (verse 19 cf. verse 14). Paul told Jew and Gentile alike that repentance was the key to spiritual life (verse 20 cf. 2:38, 3:19) and that God's power would then be available to help them live in such a way as to confirm the genuineness of their repentance (cf. Matt. 3:8).

So, because he offered salvation to the Gentiles as well as the Jews, the Jews were angry with him and seized him in the temple – even trying to kill him (verse 21 cf. 21:27,31). This was the real reason for the uproar in the temple, not the trumped-up charges presented to both Felix and Festus (cf. 24:5,6; 25:7). God has been with Paul, just as He promised, to help him keep on spreading the Good News (verse 22a). 'What's more, all this flows from the Old Testament Scriptures (e.g. Isaiah 42:6, 60:3) so I am not going against the Jews', Paul concludes (verses 22,23). Paul wishes it to be clear that he does not seek confrontation with the Jews, nor does he believe his teaching deserves their opposition.

Questions

1. Paul had been kicking 'against the goads' (verse 14). Why do we fight what we know to be right? What is God telling us to do which we keep resisting? How can we get help?

2. Paul's message is about forgiveness (verse 18). Do we always feel forgiven? Why is it important to know we are forgiven? Why is it important to forgive others?

3. Paul was glad of 'God's help' (verse 22). List some occasions when you were glad of God's help. How can you cope when God does not seem to help? In what practical ways can you be God's help to somebody else?

Acts 26:24-32

Agrippa Responds

Paul's speech is interrupted by Festus. Agrippa responds cautiously, but they all know he is innocent of any crime which deserves imprisonment or death.

Festus can contain himself no longer – he interrupts Paul in full flow (verse 24). How anyone can put his life at risk by believing that a dead man is alive, seems beyond Festus' ability to understand. He would not have followed the logic of most of Paul's speech but he would have been amazed at all the fuss generated by these religious ideas. He was a practical man and would see belief as a private thing: hardly something to get enthusiastic about and certainly not worth getting killed for! No wonder he thinks Paul is crazy.

Paul assures Festus that he is not mad, but that his words are honest and sensible (verse 25). Agrippa would be aware of the Old Testament material and have heard about the life and ministry of Jesus some thirty years earlier (verse 26). Paul has the nerve to call Agrippa as a witness for his position (verse 27); Agrippa may well 'believe the prophets' but he is not about to admit it publicly! Instead, he parries Paul's question with one of his own – is Paul really trying to persuade him to be a Christian in the course of one 'short' presentation of the gospel (verse 28)? Paul does not know how long it will take; he just knows that he wants Agrippa (and all these influential listeners) to discover what he has, so they can be Christians like he is – apart of course from being in chains (verse 29)!

Perhaps Agrippa is feeling convicted (the whole conversation has taken a very 'personal' turn in the last few minutes); he stands up (verse 30) to indicate that he considers the discussion at an end.

As King Agrippa, his sister and Governor Festus discuss the matter privately, they all agree on Paul's innocence (verse 31). He may be a little crazy, but he is not guilty of the charges brought against him. Agrippa is now in a better position to help Festus with his report, which needs to be sent with Paul to Rome (cf. 25:26). Paul is legally innocent and on that basis could be set free (verse 32); but of course it would be risky politically (see comments on 25:11), and anyway, Paul seems determined to go to Rome. His appeal to Caesar looks like being the thing which is used to fulfil Paul's ambition (19:21) as well as God's purpose for him (23:11).

Questions

1. *Do any of your non-Christian friends or neighbours think you are crazy (see verse 24)? Why do some people find the Christian faith so difficult to believe? Is Christian faith just a 'crutch' for the psychologically weak?*

2. *Paul thought his faith 'true and reasonable' (verse 25). Do you think your faith is reasonable? Can you defend what you believe? What evidence is there for the truth of Christianity.*

3. *Could you 'persuade' someone about the truth of Christianity (see verse 26)? Can you present the gospel clearly, in a couple of minutes? What are the basic elements of the Christian message which non-Christians need to hear?*

Acts 27:1–12

Journey to Rome

Paul is finally on his way to Rome, sent by Governor Festus. The first part of the trip is slow going because of the weather.

After a long two year wait, with trials under Governors Felix and Festus, Paul is at last going to Rome. He had 'appealed to Rome' (25:12), arrangements had been made, and he is finally making the trip. There were a number of other prisoners who needed to be escorted under armed guard (either to Rome or one of the cities on the way) and Paul joined them aboard ship (verse 1). Festus handed Paul over to Julius, giving him his written report on the situation (cf. 25:26,27).

Luke joins Paul on the ship (verse 2 'we') which is heading back to its base in Asia Minor. Aristarchus travels with them (cf. Col 4:10), perhaps as an aide for Paul, perhaps as another prisoner who gets converted on the voyage, we cannot know for certain. What we do know is that this section of Acts reflects Dr. Luke's eyewitness account of the journey. Here we have descriptive history at its best – written up later from the journal Luke would have kept, day by day. His description of the trade winds, general weather conditions, local ports, etc. is amazingly accurate – in a style almost like a modern documentary.

After a seventy mile journey north they dock at Sidon (verse 3) where Paul is allowed to meet with local Christians. No doubt he encouraged them in their faith just as he had at Tyre, Sidon's sister city, on his way to Jerusalem (21:3–5), and they gave him food and other necessities for a long sea voyage. On leaving Sidon, they began a frustratingly slow journey north and west (the wind was in the wrong direction (verse 4)). Eventually they made it to Myra, 150 miles to the northwest of Cyprus (verse 5). Julius had no difficulty finding a ship going to Italy in this busy port, and had his party transferred to it (verse 6). Once again sailing conditions were difficult, and progress very slow. (A 350 mile journey – Myra to Fair Havens – apparently takes weeks, instead of days, on a route which is almost twice the normal distance (verses 7,8)).

As autumn becomes winter (the day of Atonement had passed, so they may have been sailing in October) sailing becomes hazardous in this part of the Mediterranean (verse 9). Paul advises them to wait in port (verse 10) but the owner obviously wishes to deliver his cargo promptly ('time is money') and the pilot thinks it may be risky but not impossible (verse 11). They decide to sail for Crete, and harbour there for the winter (verse 12).

Questions

1. Luke tells what he sees (verse 1 'we'). Do you think this is a reliable account? How do you know that the Bible, in general, is accurate and reliable? Why is its accuracy important?

2. This journey must have frustrated Paul. How do you cope when progress (in church? at work?) is slower than you want? Why is patience so essential in the Christian life? How can we develop patience?

3. Notice how kind Julius is to Paul (verse 3). How do we relate to those we have authority over? – at home? at work? How would we like to be treated by those who have authority over us?

Acts 27:13–26

A Violent Storm

Ignoring Paul's advice, the ship sails straight into a storm! God shows Paul that despite the awful sea conditions, none of their lives will be lost.

Paul was a seasoned traveller, with some experience of Mediterranean conditions. Despite this, his advice was over-ruled by an impatient ship-owner and an over-optimistic pilot (verse 11). A light breeze from the south (verse 13) tempted them out of the harbour, along the Crete coast ... straight into a hurricane (verse 14)! They were completely at its mercy, driven south and west across the sea towards Africa (verse 15). They managed to drag the small lifeboat which they were towing, on board; thanks to an amount of shelter from a little island (verse 16).

Once away from the island, back in the full force of the hurricane, they secure the ship as best they can. The cargo is tossed over-board and a day later they even get rid of all the ship's equipment which was not absolutely essential (verses 17–19). It was not possible to get their bearings from the sun or stars (blotted out by the storm) and even the most experienced sailor had given up hope (verse 20).

Paul must have shared the general view that things were pretty bleak, although he would have been trying to hold on to what he believed God had promised him (23:11). In confirmation of this, an angel appears to him, repeating God's promise and also guaranteeing the safety of all the crew and passengers (verse 24). The Apostle, encouraged and strengthened by the angelic visitation, stands to speak to his travelling companions (verse 21a). He begins with a little self-congratulatory crowing (verse 21 'I told you so'!), and then tells them not to lose heart. The ship will be destroyed, but none of them will lose their lives (verse 22). The angel has assured Paul about this fact, along with the certainty of his ultimate arrival in Rome.

Paul is no stranger to angelic visits, visions and supernatural experiences which provide guidance and assurance for him (cf. 16:9, 18:9, 23:11). He knows that these words can be relied on – what has been said, will happen (verse 25)! It is this certainty and deep dependency on God which marks Paul out from all around him. Twice he urges them to keep up their courage (verses 22,25), not on the basis of his sea-faring knowledge but on the basis of his confidence in God! They put their trust in this, even when they did get *shipwrecked* on a remote island (verse 26).

Questions

1. *What parts of the world are characterised by a lack of hope (see verse 20)? What situations cause this? How can we help provide hope for the hopeless?*

2. *God can be relied on to do what He says (verse 25). How can we remind ourselves about this? Why do we find it so hard to trust God? What other Bible passages show us how trustworthy God is?*

3. *Is courage missing from our Christian experience (see verses 22,25)? What sort of things make us afraid? Why do so many people have 'phobias' of various kinds? What can we do about it?*

Acts 27:27–44

Shipwrecked!

The ship is driven aground by the storm and destroyed, despite all the efforts to save it. Everyone made it safely to the shore.

The storm had been raging for about two weeks, when the sailors began to feel that they were approaching land (verse 27). Their suspicions proved accurate when they took soundings of the water's depth; they quickly found themselves with less than thirty metres beneath them (verse 28). Not wanting to be driven onto rocks (especially at night) they threw four anchors from the stern and prayed for the dawn to break (verse 29). The sailors selfishly planned to abandon their passengers to a watery grave, getting away themselves in the lifeboat (verse 30). Paul knew that when daylight came all the skill of the sailors would be needed to navigate the ship closer to the shore. He alerted Julius to the danger and their cowardly desertion was thwarted (verses 31,32). This time the centurion follows Paul's advice (cf. verse 11).

Paul urges them to eat some food. Panic and pressure of work (not to mention sea-sickness!) had left them all very weak. They will need strength for the swim to shore. Paul takes some food, says grace, and begins to eat. Encouraged by this example, they all have a meal, and then throw everything else which can be moved, over the side (verses 33–38). They will need the ship to be as light as possible for the difficult approach to land. With 276 people on board there is enough human weight, without needing to carry any 'excess luggage'.

When light comes they can see land but they do not recognise it; there

217

is a sandy shore-line where it may be possible to get on land safely (verse 39). They let the sea keep the four anchors they had tossed out the night before, hoisted a small sail and tried to run aground on the beach (verse 40). They actually struck a sand-bar, got stuck with the bow trapped in the muddy sand beneath the surface, and the ship began to break up (verse 41). The soldiers wanted to kill the prisoners but Julius is especially keen to save Paul, so prevents this occurring (verses 42,43). As the stern of the ship breaks up behind them, the swimmers are encouraged to get to land. The non-swimmers were to grab anything which would float and struggle to the shore, clinging to their homemade 'rafts' (verse 44). Luke is quick to tell us that despite this undignified (not to say dangerous!) exit from the ship, not a single life is lost (verse 44b).

Questions

1. What qualities of leadership can you discover from Paul's example in this passage? Why do we need these abilities in the church today? How can we encourage and train leaders of this quality?

2. Paul told them to eat (verse 33). This does not seem very 'spiritual' advice! Is 'practical' the opposite of 'spiritual'? Shouldn't he have told them to pray? How can Christians develop this 'feet-on-the-ground' common sense?

3. Paul faces death from the storm (verse 20) and from the soldiers (verse 42)! Why is death a cause of such fear? How can we prepare to face our own death? How can we help our loved ones cope with death?

Acts 28:1–10

Safely on Land

They have been shipwrecked on Malta. The islanders are very hospitable and Paul has an opportunity for his healing ministry, after the Governor's father is healed.

The ship had been blown about 500 miles west from its last harbour (Fair Havens) and arrived at the island of Malta (verse 1). There would have been great relief at their escape from the hurricane, but some anxiety about whether or not the natives on this strange island would be friendly. They were! A large fire was built by them to help the 276 casualties avoid the consequences of exposure on a very wet and cold morning (verse 2). Paul, despite his leadership role among them and the prophetic insight which had assured them of their safety, helps collect wood for the fire. He does not assume any airs and graces or refuse to help practically because of his position or status. As he served in this humble way, a snake sank its fangs into Paul's hand (verse 3).

The snake had obviously been asleep (or close to death, from the cold?); and disturbed by the heat from the fire, had roused itself to strike at Paul. The superstitious islanders saw divine judgement in this – he may have escaped what the gods had in store for him at sea, but their plans cannot be thwarted; they send a snake to kill him on land (verse 4) – but Paul shakes this poisonous snake off into the fire and is unharmed (verse 5). The people watch this 'murderer' for hours to see if the poison will take effect, and when it does not, they assume that the 'murderer' is in fact a 'god'! (verse 6 cf. 14:11–13 for the same conclusion about Paul, but more dramatically).

Once all the 276 are accounted for, the Governor of the island (Publius) welcomes them onto his estate until accommodation can be found on the island. This process of providing food and lodging for 276 people for the winter months, takes three days (verse 7) – a remarkably efficient operation.

The father of Publius had been confined to bed with a serious illness (perhaps 'Malta fever', from a virus found in goats' milk on the island); Paul volunteered to pray with the sick man, and he was healed (verse 8). This miracle prompted others to bring their sick friends to Paul (and possibly also to doctor Luke) and he exercised a significant healing ministry on the island (verse 9). Despite all the tiredness from the long journey to Rome, a strange island, an exhausting storm, a brush with death in the shipwreck and the snake-bite ... Paul is still ready to be used by God. No wonder the islanders were so generous when the time came to leave (verse 10)!

Questions

1. *The passage describes kindness to strangers (verses 2,7). Who are the 'strangers' in our community? Would you use your home for homeless people, on a temporary basis? Would you let someone borrow your car? Share your food? Take your coat? (cf. Luke 6:30,31).*

2. *Notice Paul's humility (verse 3a). Why is humility so important? Why do we like to be noticed? How can we kill our pride, and so become usable by God.*

3. *Paul is always on duty. Do we take our Christian commitment seriously, 'in sickness and in health'? On holiday? In very busy periods? When we are tired or fed up? Don't you think Paul had earned a rest?*

Acts 28:11-16

Arriving in Rome

After spending the winter on Malta, Julius and his prisoners set sail for Italy. Paul is warmly welcomed throughout southern Italy, and arrives safely in Rome.

It was extremely difficult for sailing ships in the winter months in this part of the Mediterranean. Weather conditions would have made a journey before February close to impossible. Julius would have been keen to get his prisoners to Rome, but not keen enough to want to face another storm! They probably left Malta during early February and made their way on an Egyptian ship to Sicily, eighty miles to the north. Luke draws our attention to the figurehead which represented Gemini. These 'heavenly twins' (verse 11) were supposed to protect from storm and disaster at sea. Paul must have had a wry smile when he saw this maritime good-luck charm; he would continue to put his trust in a God who really could protect from storms (cf. 27:24)!

The journey to Syracuse was completed in a day, but a combination of bad weather and unloading of cargo kept them in port for another 72 hours (verse 12). When a favourable south wind arrived they travelled to Rhegium (a harbour in the 'toe' of Italy); and on the next day set off on the 180 mile journey up the coast to Puteoli (verse 13). At this point, Paul's journey by boat came to an end – just 140 miles short of his final destination.

Puteoli was a significant city and already had a small number of Christians. They were not slow in welcoming Paul to their city, and a week was spent together in teaching, fellowship and encouragement (verse 14 cf. brothers in Sidon 27:3). News of Paul's arrival in Italy had reached the church in Rome and they sent a delegation to give Paul a hero's welcome (verse 15). About 43 miles from Rome at the Forum of Appius and again 33 miles from Rome at Three Taverns, there are scenes of joy, greeting, welcome and fellowship. Julius must have been amazed by all this. He already knew that Paul was no ordinary prisoner, but the strength of Christian brotherhood (between people who had never met!) would have staggered him. Paul is delighted and strengthened by all this love from Italian Christians.

Paul finally arrived in Rome (verse 16) and was allowed to live on his own, in his own accommodation, though guarded by a soldier. This special treatment was no doubt obtained because of Paul's Roman citizenship, the positive nature of the letter from Festus and the glowing tribute that must have come from Julius. This mild form of house arrest gave him great freedom.

Questions

1. *Some sailors trusted in Gemini (verse 11). Why are horoscopes so popular today? Why are they dangerous? What can we do about their influence?*

2. *Paul had support from Christians (verses 14,15). In what ways is the help we get from other Christians different from any help we might get from non-Christians? How can Christians who have never met before have such close relationships so quickly?*

3. *Paul arrived in Rome at last (verse 16). Do you think there was any sense of anti-climax? How do you feel after achieving something important – let down? Bored? Empty? Why do we sometimes feel like this, after getting what we thought we wanted?!*

Acts 28:17–22

Paul and the Jewish Leaders

Wasting no time, Paul asked to meet with the Jewish leaders to explain his presence in Rome. They are not openly hostile, more curious to hear from Paul first-hand.

After just three days in Rome, Paul wishes to put his case before the leading Jews in the city (verse 17a). It was his custom to visit the synagogue as soon as he arrived in a town (cf. 13:14, 14:1) but his house arrest made this very difficult; on this occasion they would have to come to him. Using the normal greeting ('men, brothers'), he begins to explain his presence in Rome to them. He is anxious to reassure them about his loyalty as a Jew. He has not done anything to damage the Jewish people or been deliberately acting against the established traditions (verse 17b). Despite this, he was arrested in Jerusalem and tried by the Romans, though they came to believe he was innocent (verse 18) of any significant crime (cf. 25:7, 26:31,32).

When the Jews in Judea were resistant to Paul's freedom, he felt that he had to invoke his right as a Roman citizen to be tried by Caesar (verse 19). He is at pains to point out that this was simply to protect his own life, not to bring a counter-charge against the Jews. Paul believes that his presence in Rome is due to a disagreement about the 'hope of Israel' (verse 20) that is, a dispute relating to the Messiah. Every Jew looked forward to the day when God's great deliverer would come; it was a completely orthodox expectation. The difference between Paul and his accusers was that he believed that this 'hope' had been fulfilled in Jesus, and they did not!

In response to this initial explanation, the leaders of the Jewish community say that they have had no correspondence from Jerusalem about him and that Jewish visitors to Rome have not brought any negative reports to them (verse 21). This is difficult to believe, even with communication being slow in the ancient world. Perhaps they are being incredibly diplomatic because they feel very vulnerable in Rome as a mistrusted minority. Perhaps they want to maintain a low profile and not get involved in any controversy. Paul can never have been treated so respectfully by Jewish leaders!

Whatever the reasons for their non-hostile response, they are curious to hear first-hand from this Christian missionary. Everyone seems to be talking about Christianity (verse 22) and they are keen to discover what the fuss is all about.

Questions

1. *Paul has not been disloyal to his Jewish heritage (verse 17). Why is loyalty so important to him? How do we demonstrate 'loyalty' – to Christ? To the church? To our partner? To the family? To our country?*

2. *Paul claimed Jesus was the Messiah (see verse 20). Why do you think this was hard for the Jews to believe? What Old Testament passages point to Jesus as the Messiah? How would you go about persuading a Jew about Jesus today?*

3. *When does 'diplomacy' become lying (see verse 21)? How do we know the difference? Can 'silence' ever be a lie? Is it alright to lie to protect someone you love?*

Acts 28:23–31

The Gospel is Preached

Paul explains his position fully to the Jewish leaders. There is a mixed response. Paul continues to preach to everyone who will listen!

The leaders of the Jews arranged to come back to hear Paul on a more convenient occasion. When they returned, the delegation had increased in size; interest in this 'Christian', this leading light of a new 'sect' (verse 22) was obviously substantial. Paul must have been staying in some spacious accommodation, in order to entertain them all. For a whole day he tried to persuade them about life in God's kingdom (verse 23). This was also the theme of the risen Jesus to the first disciples (1:3). He worked hard to demonstrate that Moses and the Prophets had all pointed to Jesus as Messiah; that he was not a believer in a new religion, simply that he was enjoying what God had promised would happen.

It would have been a great delight to Paul that some of these men of authority in the Jewish synagogue, came to faith in Christ (verse 24 cf. Crispus in 18:8). Of course, there were some who refused to believe because of stubbornly closed minds ... and perhaps the majority were just unsure what to make of it all. Certainly there was division among them, just as there had been at the Sanhedrin trial in Jerusalem (verse 25a cf. 23:9). The final straw for many of them came when Paul made his closing two points.

Firstly, he quoted Isaiah 6:9 to them. The prophets had always known how stubborn the Jews would be and how they would fail to recognise the Messiah (verses 26,27). Secondly, this meant that Paul now had the freedom to take his message to the Gentiles, so that they could enjoy all the benefits of God's salvation (verse 28 cf. 9:15, 13:46–48). This was more than these Jews could take and they slipped out before they heard anything even more shocking.

For two years Paul was allowed to live comfortably in his rented accommodation and had no problem receiving visitors whenever they came (verse 30). Luke concludes his book with a verse of encouragement and confidence. Paul's physical confinement did not mean that the preaching of the gospel was inhibited. Far from it. He was able to speak without fear, boldly explaining his beliefs and pointing his visitors to the Jesus, who was both Lord and Christ (verse 31 cf. 2:36). This truth was proclaimed to Jew and Gentile alike. It was a message which would be preached all over the world (1:8) until the Jesus Paul loved returned (cf. 1:11).

Questions

1. *Are there any individuals (or groups of people) who we do not really want to hear the gospel (cf. 'Gentiles')? Should we evangelise people of other religions or just those with no faith? Do we need foreign missionaries any more? Why?*

2. *Paul got a mixed response (verse 24). What kind of response do we get? What should the church do to encourage those who believe? How can we respond to those who don't? Should we move on to other people or keep trying?*

3. *Paul took every opportunity to evangelise (verse 31). Why was evangelism such a priority for him? How can we make it more of a priority for ourselves? Why should we? How can we go about it?*

Whatever happened to Paul?

Nobody knows the answer to this question, although there have been many attempts to discover the truth. Some believe that at the end of the two years (28:30) Paul was tried by Caesar and then executed. But if this is so, it is hard to explain Luke's silence about the matter and harder still to explain some of the material in Paul's letters, particularly the letters to Timothy.

Paul was probably freed after two years because the case against him was weak (cf. 26:31,32) and his accusers had failed to turn up in Rome. He thought he might get thrown to the lions, but avoided this fate (2 Tim. 4:17) and may have had the opportunity to re-visit some of the churches he had planted. He may even have made his way to Spain, fulfilling a strong desire to preach the gospel there (Rom. 15:24,28). He could well have been re-arrested at a time when the Roman authorities were less sympathetic to Christianity (e.g. after the great fire of Rome [A.D. 64] which emperor Nero blamed the Christians for starting). It seems most likely that Paul was martyred between A.D. 65-68 in the Nero-inspired persecutions.

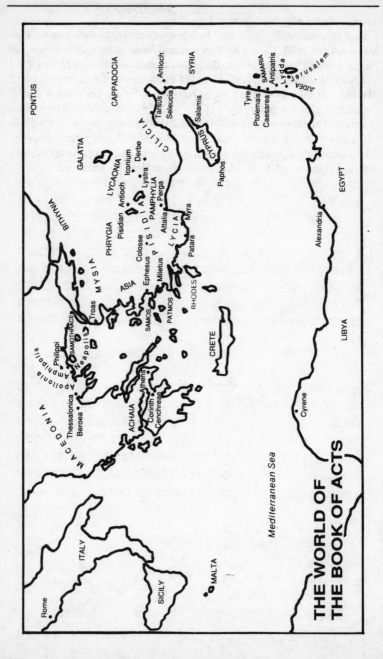

THE WORLD OF
THE BOOK OF ACTS

Also available from Crossway Books

PROPHET
A NOVEL
Frank E. Peretti

' You will know the truth, and the truth will set you free' (John 8: 32)

John Barrett, anchorman for 'NewsSix at Five', the city's most watched newscast, has a problem. His comfortable, successful world is being jarred to breaking point. He's caught his producer skewing a story to fit her own prejudices, then lying to cover her tracks – and she appears to be hiding something much bigger. His father's 'accidental' death suddenly isn't looking so accidental. Carl, his estranged son, has returned to challenge his integrity and probe to find the man behind the TV image. The supposedly professional and objective newsroom is now divided and fighting over Truth. And what are these mysterious 'voices' Barrett is hearing ...?

Once again, master storyteller **Frank Peretti** has woven a prophetic tale for our times. *Prophet* carries all the hallmarks of Frank's blockbusting fiction – plenty of edge-of-the-seat action, nail-biting suspense, breakneck pacing, and blow-you-out-of-the-water spiritual impact. But more than this, it penetrates to the very heart of a vast struggle that threatens to tear our society to pieces, the struggle over which vision of moral authority will define our nation.

THE CHURCH THAT TURNED THE WORLD UPSIDE DOWN

Roy Clements

So great an impact did the early Christians make on those around them that people said that they had turned the world upside down.

We too should make the same impression, at home, at work, at leisure. We often feel intimidated by the task, so how much more should the early church have had cause to be frightened – a tiny band of believers in a hostile world. Yet within a few years the church had grown to thousands across the Roman empire.

The lessons they learned are as applicable today as ever. In this masterful study of Acts, Roy Clements shows us how we too can turn the world upside down.

Roy Clements is the Pastor of Eden Chapel in Cambridge. Well known as a speaker at many events, he is also the author of several books. He is married to Jane, with three children.

A PASSION FOR HOLINESS
J. I. Packer

Changing our lives for the better

The sequel to *Keep in Step with the Spirit*.

'This will take our best thinking and our most faithful living.'
Richard Foster

'No one is better qualified to address this call.'
Chuck Colson

As Christians succumb more and more to materialism, holiness is becoming the forgotten virtue of the Church. Yet, as the Bible makes clear, holiness is high on God's priorities for his people.

J. I. Packer brings us back to where God wants us to be. He shows us that holiness is nothing less than a lifelong passion for loving God and following his ways.

J. I. Packer is Professor of Systematic and Historical Theology at Regent College, Vancouver, Canada, and has also held posts in his native Britain. Dr. Packer is the author of numerous best-sellers including *Knowing God, Keep in Step with the Spirit* and most recently *Among God's Giants*.

MY PATH OF PRAYER
Edited by David Hanes

Personal experiences of God

David Watson, J. I. Packer, Derick Bingham, Michael Baughen, Edward England, Jean Darnall, J. Oswald Sanders, Selwyn Hughes, Phyllis Thompson, Jean Wilson, Richard Wurmbrand.

'Unusually helpful contribution to the needs of ordinary battle-scarred Christians.'

Michael Green

Here is a book that will encourage us to pray, based on the personal experiences of some leading Christians. By discovering the secrets of their prayer lives we learn to approach our Heavenly Father more easily ourselves.

This classic book, now reissued, will speak to you today.

SWEET AND SOUR PORK
THE JOYS AND PAINS OF A PRODIGAL SON
Jeff Lucas

With honesty and lots of humour, Jeff Lucas offers us answers to some down to earth questions.

- Can we find contentment in life?
- What is repentance all about?
- Why do I still feel guilty when I know that God has forgiven me?
- Is it fun being a Christian?

Discover how Father God has invited each one of us to a very special celebration.

'This is my kind of book. It has that very rare quality of being profoundly biblical, at the same time as being extremely readable, down to earth and practical. I can honestly say that my only regret is that it wasn't written 20 years ago when I was first a Christian. It is witty, enlightening, compassionate and deeply challenging. If you're anything like me, *Sweet and Sour Pork* will make you laugh, make you think and help you to see both God and yourself that much more clearly.'

Steve Chalke

'This book deals a major blow to the sort of Christianity which has little to do with Christ. It is a must for those who feel they have failed and can't start again, have sinned and can't find a way back, have lost faith and are unsure of the Father's welcome.'

Gerald Coates

Jeff Lucas is a regular Spring Harvest speaker with an international teaching ministry. He and his family live in Chichester, where he works with Revelation Church and the Pioneer Team.